The Last Dragon

Dragon

A Triathlon Journey

By Jimmy Patterson

Foreword

"A ship in harbour is safe, but that is not what ships are built for."

John A Shedd

Contents

Origin Story

I've been told that the best place to start is the beginning, and that takes me back to being a youngster, growing up in Cardiff, Wales. Much to the frustration of my active family and no doubt some PE teachers over the early years, I was never that keen on sport. I was tall for my age, pretty quick on foot and not too bad at sports requiring hand/eye coordination. Unfortunately I let Asthma become an excuse to not take sport any further and decided to release my teenage energy towards amateur dramatics. Therefore anything sport related was met with fleeting interest and after high school there was little to no physical activity taking place in my life other than drinking games and chasing girls.

I am unable to pinpoint the precise moment and I can't quite find the memory in my head as to why, but mid September 2009, at the tender age of 23, I decided to buy a pair of running trainers and go for a run around the block of my neighborhood. This was pretty impulsive for me, having not run for any other reason than catching an approaching bus, that was about it. Now, when I say "go for a run" what I really mean is jog, and by jog I actually mean trot. The distance? A grand total of 370m (0.23 miles). It was hardly worth measuring, but it was a start, and I had no idea of where those first steps would take me. Completing the short lap of the neighbourhood block was a small goal, and to be honest, it was enough. After huffing and puffing my way around the pavement for only a few minutes, my body went into total shock. My chest tightened, my heart rate went through the roof and body parts reacting to movement they have not done for a long time, but that burst of adrenaline firing through my veins felt good.

After years of bumbling through university, working jobs with no direction, travelling to places unknown and ultimately drinking far too much booze, eating too much shite and generally abusing my body, I actually felt alive for the first time in a long while. That might have been down to the feeling of my heart exploding, or blood reaching dormant parts of my brain, but it felt like I had a new purpose, a way I could turn the world off around me and enter my own zone, without the pressure or questioning from anyone else. I wasn't quite becoming a runner, but I was slowly undoing all the neglect to my body and heading in the right direction.

Just a foreword before we move any further. One thing that is consistent in the world of swimming, cycling and running, is the inconsistency of metrics. Ultimately it comes down to preference, but what metric to measure speed, distance and pace in can divide the closest of friends. On UK roads we use imperial measurements with speed and distance measured in miles. Our European neighbours use the metric system with metres and kilometers. The USA are with the Brits on this one, joined by a handful of other countries.

When it comes to measuring the disciplines of triathlon, it's a free for all. A 5k run sounds more aesthetically pleasing compared to the converted 3.1 miles. Have you ever heard someone say, "I'm just going for a 3.1 mile run"? The answer is no. It's the same with 10k / 6.21 miles. Cycling however splits opinion more dramatically as speeds and distances tend to be in larger numbers.

Therefore, for the purpose of this book, and keeping in line with the I-don't-know-what-I'm-doing journey, I will replicate real life and casually flit between the two. I swim in metres until the distances get larger. Cycling, in terms of distance and speed are always measured in miles unless it's referring to a shorter race. Running, as mentioned previously, is a different ball game. Running is clocked in kilometres when referring to shorter distances (5k and 10k), anything longer such as half marathons and marathons are referred to in miles.

Back to running, I was never that *good* at running, and by good I mean both fast and consistent. Maybe because of that missing competitive streak I lacked in early adolescence, but I used running as an excuse to get out of the family home. With other aspects of my life not yet clear, running was pure escapism, and although very much needed, I was clearly running away from my problems.

Running the neighbourhood block once a week soon became twice a week, and not long after, the one lap soon multiplied. Feeling better and better after each run it wasn't long until I stretched my running further to incorporate a nearby park. I was starting to enjoy the dangerous spike of increased heart rate a few days a week as it also helped balance the junk food and weekend booze I was still over consuming. However, I was in no way ready to join a running club or enter any races.

My first event came three months after lacing my runners up for the first time. I know, I know. I said I wasn't ready for a race, and this wasn't a race. It was a 5k Santa Dash around a local park in support of the British Heart Foundation. With every run I could hear my own heart pounding through my chest, and the irony wasn't lost on me.

Knowing nobody there, I arrive too early and anxiously wait for the event to start. This was the first time running in a group of any capacity and I used the fact I was wearing a full Santa costume with a fluffy white beard as a comforter, for some reason embarrassed and praying no one would recognise me. I also took an early internal boost knowing I wasn't going to finish this race last. That had nothing to do with my own ability, I was still a plodder of a jogger, but there were young children and families of all abilities at the start line. It was great to see, and also a great opportunity to experience running in a big group.

After a brief safety announcement, (wondering what could possibly go wrong at a 5k Santa Dash), the klaxon blows and off I trot. It didn't take long to meander through the slower starters and relax into a gentle pace, embrace the occasion and find a suitable compromise with the synthetic beard tied to my face. As first events go, this was ideal. There was no pressure, no expectation and all kept under the radar, nobody knew I was running this event, it was all for me. I crossed the line in a time not worth remembering, but feeling overwhelmingly delighted of what I achieved, proudly wearing my plastic medal with honor. It was my first timed 5k, in a group of people and I needed more of it. Fortunately for me there were plenty of opportunities to get my new fix; but I still lacked the desire, motivation and maybe the confidence to take it seriously.

The next few years were filled with local street runs of varying distances at speeds that went unrecorded. This was before the obsessive world of synced Garmin watches, Strava segments and personal bests (or personal records), where that extra element of motivation is now commonly harvested. Running motivation came in waves, and without a steady group of "active" friends, no balls to join a club and temptations coming in from different angles, I squandered my youth, and maybe my potential.

In 2010 I did however manage to complete the Cardiff Half Marathon in what was, at the time, a huge achievement for me. During the first year of intermittent casual running I didn't have the belief that I was capable of running the 13.1 miles of a half marathon, but the opportunity to take part in the event to support the excellent charity Macmillan was all too appealing. The thought of running for someone in need was the motivation to sign up to the event. That was half the battle as training and preparation for the 13.1 miles were futile. With no plan I trained on how I felt. If I didn't want to run, I didn't. If it was raining, I made an excuse. Stretching, strength work and intervals were nonexistent. Based on what I put into training, I wasn't expecting to get much out of the race. I was just making up the numbers.

The whole spectacle and occasion of running around my home city with street lined supporters cheering your every step was magical. You're not allowed to stop; you are encouraged to keep moving at every possible moment until you finish, it was overwhelming and I ate up the atmosphere.

Crossing that finish line, after 2 hours and 15 minutes, I was rewarded with my first medal made of metal, a chocolate biscuit and paralysing cramp! I'm convinced it was the worst pain I had ever experienced, it felt like my quads were being twisted off my legs and the only way to prevent that torture was to stretch in a way to alleviate the pain. In true Murphy's Law my hamstrings wanted to join in the fun and decided to add to the cramp now in all areas of both legs. I had only hobbled a half marathon, why was this happening to me!? Yes it may have been the furthest distance I had ever run, but I raised some cash for a charity and I just wanted to revel in my accomplishment.

Instead I was rendered useless for what seemed like an eternity, unable to hold a conversation and walk unaided. Fortunately my parents were on hand to carry me back to the car. The main cause of cramp is dehydration and it wouldn't be the last time I would have to battle with this debilitating pain as it's still a few years until I find the wonder of salt tablets and electrolytes.

Between 2011 and 2015 I took part in two additional half marathons and three 10k's all in Cardiff with a consistency of a mid pack finisher that I was happy with. The events were completed with the intention to just finish. I didn't care about time, I enjoyed being a part of something bigger. I wasn't invested enough to train hard as I still didn't think I could finish much faster.

The game changer however was parkrun, which I'm sure you have heard, seen or have even taken part in by now as it's been around for a while, globally. For those who have not heard of parkrun I'll briefly explain. It is simply a timed, 5k run/jog/walk every Saturday morning, normally about 09:00. All for free. Your times are recorded and posted online every week, charting positions, times and age group statistics. Again, all for free.

For me, parkrun brought about some routine, an excuse to not overindulge the previous night and with it came a newfound appreciation for other runners. Without sounding like a creep it was great to see all shapes, sizes, ages and abilities turn up each and every week, rain or shine, looking to better themselves. I was part of that group, I am testiment to how addictively motivating parkrun can be.

There were elite runners with big goals in sight, sprinting away from the get-go and finishing within 17 minutes. There were first timers who were slower, but with just as important goals. Getting to the start line is a win in my book, it took a while, but I was starting to see how powerful and life changing running was.

Parkrun isn't labeled as a race but let's be honest, it totally is! It's a race against yourself; you turn up and give it your best. Who doesn't love a personal best and some evidence of progress? The more you attend, the more likely you will find yourself running with and against the same people who are of similar pace. Those people can become your friends, your enemies, or even *frenemies*, although all light hearted.

By the end of 2015 Cardiff parkrun (now referred to as Blackweir) were averaging 500 runners each week, and with national parkrun records being smashed frequently, Cardiff was hotting up to be the fastest route around. It also meant that with the increasing demand the need for additional locations around Cardiff was considered necessary. There are now four locations within a two mile radius that attract a healthy amount of runners each week.

Even so, Cardiff parkrun (Blackweir) was still growing in popularity with average attendees topping around 750 each week, maxing out a record breaking 1192 runners during 2018! Parkrun tourists were coming from far and wide and it was great to give a warm welcome to any newbie. The love was reciprocated when I ventured outside of Wales to take part in different events while on holiday and weekend trips away. I found my way to a few parkruns in Scotland, Ireland and even Canada. The ethos is identical to what I was used to, and such a welcoming community to be part of.

Lastly, but no means least, it would be sacrilegious to mention parkrun without a special shout out to the volunteers. They are the true heroes that make this free event run smoothly. Setting up, directing, marshalling, counting and packing up. 1000's of runners wouldn't have a parkrun if it wasn't for them. Every volunteer is your best friend, but if you attend in the future, please don't forget your barcode. Plead as you may, there is nothing they can do if you forget.

2015 was drawing to a close and I hadn't really achieved anything notable. I had recently acquired an allotment with two friends and that seemed to absorb a lot of time. As much as I did and still do enjoy pottering around a slightly neglected looking plot of land, it was definitely a slower pace of activity. A typical Saturday morning involved a 09:00 parkrun, followed by a sausage and bacon roll down the allotment with a donut chaser. I would spend a few hours digging, weeding and general gardening, which prompted an afternoon nap in front of the TV before sorting myself out for a night of heavy drinking and questionable dancing. The least we talk about Sunday the better. With all the potential positives that running offers, I was still stuck in a rut with a lack of enthusiasm to get out and do more. I needed another intervention.

Uncharted Territory

It was a dark and cold Monday evening in November and after a weekend typically filled with alcohol and questionable decisions, I had the overwhelming impulse to buy a bike. Although it seemed a spur of the moment urge, I'm sure I wasn't still drunk, I felt the universe was calling and I couldn't ignore it any longer, this was the intervention I needed. Call it a divine intervention, because it was the spark that ignited the next chapter of my life, and maybe saved it.

Other than my infrequent chest pains, asthma, a questionable relationship with alcohol, dodgy knees and bad eyesight, I was fit and healthy. A number of friends have been riding the cycling bandwagon for a while and swear true that it was better than running. So combining my casual love for a physical challenge, a financial situation which allowed me to purchase a decent set of wheels and the support of some pushy pedal pushers, it was happening. It was keeping up with the Joneses in full swing, I knew it, but I didn't care.

There were two options with buying a bike, purchase one myself or use the government's health initiative and take advantage of the Cycle to Work scheme. The latter seemed like the obvious choice as I was able to pay the bike off in monthly installments through my salary. The format was allowing tax free purchases up to £1,000 to be spent on a bicycle and accessories, which to me seemed reasonable. Instead of looking into the scheme to further my knowledge and to work out salary logistics, I was straight to the interweb to heighten my excitement of buying a bike. That was pretty much a bad move, the first of many when it came to cycling.

I learnt straight away that cycling at any level other than casual is so damn expensive! My online search criteria soon filtered *out* carbon frames, disk brakes and top end group sets. Even with a restricted search result I was still clueless, my bicycle knowledge at this stage was limited to knowing the number of wheels I required.

I needed help, and it was time to get some backing from someone who knew a little more than the difference between a mountain bike and a road bike, my good friend Thomas.

Tom had made the decision to get onboard the road bike train since the beginning of the summer and found it difficult to contain his own excitement of potentially having a new bike *wanker* buddy. This trusted source of information was vital and with his wise words and experience it made not only rationalising this purchase a lot easier, but it was a great source of knowledge to lean on in the future.

A big question still remained; what bike should I purchase? I needed a bike that was modern, durable and within price range with the main objective of providing an option for a 16 mile round trip commute and some cycling further afield on the occasional weekend. The search results still return a myriad of options. Call it lazy, or call it genius. But Tom bought a bike within the same parameters a few months prior and it just made sense to buy the same one. Obviously in a different colour of course!

With a bike in mind, it was time to do some more research. The majority of the week was spent watching videos, reading blogs, searching websites and trying to update my knowledge on my new fitness venture. I still didn't have a clue, but I did start to see what my money was going to buy, or more so, what it *wasn't* buying. My first bike as an adult was becoming a reality; a 2015

Specialized Allez Sport was only a cycle scheme away.

With the boss on board and the cycle scheme in the process of being sorted out, the next few days were spent receiving ill-fitting cycling apparel and equipment. Exposing Lycra, snoods, jerseys, puncture repair kit, a pump and some gloves, this sport was already expensive and I hadn't even purchased the bike yet.

So with all the gear, no idea, and no road bike, the best thing to do was to sign up to a Velothon. Yep, you read that correctly. With no actual bike and with no idea whether I would enjoy the thing, I decided to sign up for an 85 mile cycle, taking part in the heart of South Wales. I've not turned one revolution of a pedal and I'm eyeing up some mega distances and some locally notorious climbs.

After waiting impatiently for another week finally the cycle scheme certificate gets emailed through and I'm making a b-line to the bike shop. It felt like my birthday and Christmas rolled into one big boner. It was clear to the shop owner that I had a bike in mind and that was that; "here's the bike, jump on and we'll double check the size". All the research couldn't prepare me for the first time sitting on a road bike saddle. I questioned if there was an actual seat on this bike. It's safe to say that if I wanted to protect my delicate areas those tight nappy padded tights would come to the rescue. I left the shop with a helmet, bottle, cage, inner tubes, tyre levers and a brand spanking new Specialized Allez Sport. Buzzing. Front wheel off, and it's all in the back of my three door Vauxhall Corsa.

My new baby was home and straight into a mobile phone photo shoot, mainly standing pose and against the wall but to be honest I have no idea why, it just seemed like the right thing to do. It is something that I see a lot of nowadays, and mainly on social media. Keen cyclists sharing their new bike and then a Strava ride showing exactly where they started and stopped – this tends to be the place their lovely new bike will be kept overnight, ready to be stolen. Unfortunately I have seen this far too often, and insurance companies are sometimes unwilling to pay out on grounds of undue care and attention.

The bike came with those standard cage type pedals you put your feet into, and even though it was dark (its November, it's always dark) and I had no lights, there was no way I was *not* going to get on and take it for a spin. They say you never forget how to ride a bike, and that piece of advice was ridiculously un-true. Granted I only graced the small street with a few laps but I was as wobbly as a bowl full of jelly. It also dawned early on that not only was my new sporting chapter going to be fun; it was also going to be fast! I was pleasantly surprised with how quickly the bike picked up speed, with minimal effort. I assumed it was something to do with the two skinny tires I was wobbling on. A few minutes test drive and I was back in the house taking more pointless photos, my heart still beating with excitement.

The next big test was an actual cycle. You know, a real one, on roads, wearing cycling gear and heading out further than just the block. Being the start of winter in Wales it was of course cold and with a threatening cloud formation, not the best conditions to dip my toe, but I had to start somewhere. With the wind blowing and rain in the air, my cycling buddy, who was just as nervous as me, took me on an 18 mile jaunt around some quiet, flat, coastal lanes. A relatively easy "bimble" you may think, but negotiating gears and brakes on unfamiliar handlebars with a new body position, navigating varying terrain on seemingly the thinnest wheels proved a challenge in itself. One and half hours later, I was home, knackered.

Still in my damp Lycra, drinking a brew, looking at my bike with a smile on my face I concede that I thoroughly enjoyed my first proper cycle, it was great fun and fortunately no major concerns or any incidents to put me off going out again, but not straight away. As suspected there was a slight discomfort to body parts that I guessed over time would become the norm. In short, my hands ached early on, my neck ached later on, my legs hurt the following two days but after all the waiting, the embarrassing clobber and fitness doubts I could candidly say that I was a now a cyclist. With 18 miles on the milometer the thought of the recently purchased Velothon Wales entry filled me with absolute dread and sheer excitement.

Naturally you'd think I would have ticked off some more miles on the bike soon after my first outing, but another borderline stupid idea crossed my mind and it got stuck there. That stupid idea was a Triathlon. Thinking back to this point in time is something I frequently revisit in my head. I had hobbled through a few half marathons, I had just bought a bike and clocked no more than 30 miles, and now I wanted to throw swimming into the mix.

Some triathletes, for a whole range of reasons, get to the swim/bike/run start line by *normally* building their interest from one of the three disciplines. Some are naturally strong cyclists, some are swimmers and in my case I had started with running. My interest with triathlon was mainly to satisfy a question, *what would happen?* What would happen if I signed up for a triathlon? Would I love it? Would I hate it? Where would it lead? This is now some sort of mantra I feel deep down when thinking of other challenges. What will happen? Fuck it, take my money and let's find out.

My first triathlon was in my home town of Cardiff. It would involve a 750m swim in the questionable waters of Cardiff Bay, a relatively flat 20k cycle and an equally flat 5k run partway across the barrage and back. Two of those disciplines were comfortably acceptable – I can run 5k and I could ride a bike. As with most newbie's, swimming was the leg most troubling, and just to ramp up the fear factor, it was in open water.

Again, you'd think I'd get on the bike or get in some swimming. No. I was on a roll and decided to sign up for another half marathon too. You may be thinking I was deep into some sort of early onset mid-life crisis and I'd probably agree. It was questionable decision after questionable decision, but I didn't care.

So let's just recap – without much thinking I had signed up for a trilogy of events which included a half marathon, a velothon and my first triathlon taking place in four, six and seven months respectively. What the actual fuck am I doing!?

Well they say charity starts at home, and this threesome of events was proof in the pudding. Plagiocephaly and Brachycephaly are conditions commonly known as "flat head". This is where a newborn baby's skull has twisted, deformed or squashed during birth which can result in potentially long term development issues unless treated with the use of a counteractive helmet.

Just before these challenges began, my nephew was born with a severe case of "flat head" and would develop issues growing up without the corrective shapening of a helmet. Strangely the NHS couldn't provide any support in this "cosmetic" issue but in stepped a charity called Head Start 4 Babies who kindly provided guidance and financial support towards the cost of a helmet for the little one. Fast forward, my nephew turned out just fine, he can be a little shit at times but I love him with all of my heart.

It was therefore decided that I would attempt these events and raise some cash for the charity that helped out my nephew. It was the right thing to do, and what I found early on was that as soon as the donations came in, I knew I couldn't back down; every pound was converted into motivation and determination.

It was nearing the end of the year and to be honest I had not done as much as I had wanted to in terms of training, I didn't really have a plan at this stage, and it was just a case of turning the legs and attending some parkruns. The New Year was going to be the springboard into official training, but there was an elephant in the room and that was swimming. I needed to get in the pool before the Christmas break to make sure I hadn't bitten off more than I could chew. Have I mentioned I can't swim?

So yeah, a big reveal of this story – I've not swam front crawl, or any other crawl for that matter since primary school, some 20 years prior. I've been in a swimming pool and paddled, but not swam with intent. How hard can it be, muscle memory is a thing right? There was only one way to find out how big this challenge was going to be.

Cardiff boasts a 50 metre competitive pool and also a 25 metre leisure pool, which with full of confidence I strolled straight passed, scoffing at the elderly folk splashing about, I headed towards the "real" pool. I stood on the edge of the internationally recognised 50m sized pool, wearing a pair of flower print surf shorts, and that's it, for some reason I thought this was appropriate. What a complete dick! I jumped straight in, knowing it was deep enough but not knowing how deep. I cling to the side and realise that should I get into difficulty half way across I'll have to grab onto one of the guide ropes either side of the lane. Even that was optimistic; I didn't make it past 20m before it was all too much for me. Not having a swimming cap meant that my long afro hair covered my face. Not having goggles meant the chlorine stung my open eyes. Not having a clue meant I was pretty much vertical, clawing at the water, losing energy and gasping for breath. How I wasn't dragged out by a lifeguard I'll never know. I somehow managed a full length. I pulled myself out, still gasping for air and walked towards the shallower leisure pool, tail between my legs, desperate for the old biddies to accept me, which to my relief they did.

Swimming cap, new trunks and goggles were ordered that morning, but it was a while until I was back in the pool again. To be honest the whole breathless doggy paddle episode haunted me for a while. I was in my own head, and the answer to how much I had bitten off was clear, it was a lot. So I needed a plan, and it involved swallowing my pride, going back to basics and counting.

Build Phase

In swung the New Year and while I was still finding the balls to get back into the pool the cycling continued, but even this turned out to be a slight step backwards. My new pedals, cleats and clip in shoes had arrived – I was now "clipless" which meant learning two valuable lessons – the first is that one of your bike pedals unscrews in the opposite direction to lefty-loosey-righty-tighty. It took some Class A swear words and a lot of spent energy to work that one out. The other was that stopping at traffic lights, roundabouts and junctions required some serious thought. You soon discover which your strongest foot is. The bonus lesson learnt was that "clipless" actually means that your *toes* are no longer clipped in, even though your foot *is*. The mind boggles.

I soon got used to being connected to the bike after a few short rides around the quieter side streets, practicing how to slow down, unclip, stop and start again. There is something quite satisfying about clipping in straight away and riding off. However, complacency is a bitch, as is fatigue, and those two combined will no doubt result in stacking it at the worst possible moments, normally at traffic lights in front of a van full of lads! For now, things were going well on the bike and I was keeping alive.

Two days later and with my cycle buddy we decided to head out to Barry Island, a 30 mile round trip of sunny, windy, uncharted coast road lay before us.

Gaining confidence after every mile I found the whole cycling game very much enjoyable, with the bakery pit stop being a highlight. That is the part of cycling (and later on triathlon training) that I found easy to get on board with. The amount of calories you need to fuel your activities balances the workloads perfectly. The cycle was not grueling in any way, shape or form; there were a few climbs but nothing to warrant any foul language. However, food intake is now a key consideration as the two hour cycle meant I had expended my breakfast energy (most probably a bowl of cereal and a milky brew) and my body was in need of a boost. I had started to mix in cordial to my water to add a bit of sugar to my bloodstream, but I was lacking the sustenance to keep hunger at bay. Turns out the trick to fueling while on the move during a moderately active cycle is that you can eat whatever you are willing to carry. Getting a cycling jersey with some deep pockets is a must if you're looking to carry your lunch. Alternatively planning a route with a cycle friendly café is also a smart move. For my next few rides I was stuffing pockets with high carb, sugary and salty goodies.

What I'm also finding interesting at this stage of my cycling journey is seeing familiar areas, neighborhoods and locations that I've passed plenty of times in the car but paid very little notice too. Cycling grants you more time to take in surroundings and appreciate them a little more. This is still something that I love about cycling today, there is beauty in every cycle that can be missed or ignored during a car journey.

During this time of my life I was actually working in Barry, and so the bonus of my recent jaunt to the Island was that it acted as a reconnaissance mission. Combined with the fact that I purchased this bicycle on the Cycle to Work scheme, it made sense to commit a few days to pedaling to and from the office. The benefit of having a shower on site made the day more manageable, for both my colleagues and I.

Logistically it was all a bit of a faff as I needed to plan ahead to make sure I had workable clothes in the office ready to change into after the commute. There was the need for a towel, shower gel, breakfast and lunch to consider and maybe a second set of cycling clothes should the weather change at the end of the day. I opted to prepare all of that the day prior to the planned cycle to work and leave it there ready, instead of having to cart it with me in a rucksack on the big day.

The route was different to what I tried the previous week as I decided on a more direct path. It was early, a lot colder than I'd like but also a lot quieter. After arriving at work in one piece (much to my colleague's relief), I took a shower, (again, much to my colleague's relief) and I was eating breakfast at my desk with 10 minutes to spare (much to my manager's relief). I must admit, not much work was done that day. The early start and 8 cold miles of commute rattled my energy limits. I was shagged, but as the day moved along my excitement of cycling home grew stronger, come 17:00 and I miraculously had plenty of energy to get home. Once again I decided on a different route on my return, this time taking a little longer journey as I had no time limit to get home.

Finishing at 17:00 meant I hit a shit load of traffic heading back into Cardiff. This meant a lot more stopping and starting, having to utilise bus and cycle lanes and also feeling smug about weaving (safely) between the lines of built up traffic when approaching lights, roundabouts and other junctions. It's all great fun but it does highlight the dangers of cycling and how unseen cyclists can be on the road. I made sure I was visible, having invested in both front and rear lights I insisted they were switched on even though there was plenty of natural light still available.

I'm not hating on all drivers, but there is some animosity from a minority of non-cycling drivers towards cyclists, and I'm not really sure why, but some believe it's related to the laughable "you should pay road tax to be on the road" argument. Without going too deep into the psychology of this issue, car drivers get frustrated with cyclists who don't pay "road tax", use the roads, and occasionally don't follow the rules, (jumping lights and using pavements as a shortcut to name a few).

To counter this, Road Tax is Vehicle Excise Duty and is based on emissions. Other than flatulence, a cyclist produces zero percent emissions. I do of course believe cyclists should follow the rules of the road but there is plenty of space for all road users.

Furthermore, cycling is environmentally friendly and the benefits surely outweigh the hospital admissions for health related illness.

It would be great, where possible, that all learner drivers take some sort of cycle proficiency test as part of their training. I don't know how it would work but since cycling I feel my awareness of other cyclists when *I'm* driving has improved dramatically. The way I approach a cyclist or a group ride would be a lot different to how someone who doesn't cycle would.

The cycle home was without any incident but once again I experienced the onset of cramp during the crossing of the busiest roundabout in Cardiff. I still needed to up my salt and water intake before and during any cycling. I figured I should probably stretch and do some yoga to keep loose and limber, but one step at a time.

Other than my pen pushing 9 to 5 job stopping my cycling fun, I had an enjoyable day on the bike. That evening I cracked open a beer, checked Strava and felt a great sense of achievement having cycled my first commute. Calories burnt, carbon footprint low, saddle sore inbound.

Cycling to and from work continued intermittently based on logistics, other commitments and mainly weather. At the early stages of this new commuting option it was safe to say that I was a fair weather cyclist, anything more than drizzle and I would opt against using the bike. It was a confidence thing mostly; cycling on skinny tires while clipped in took a while to get used to. However my bike did see water frequently through washing it. It seemed like after every ride it picked up dust, dirt and muck which after a while would no doubt start hindering the performance of my bike. I assumed there was one way to wash a bike, with washing up liquid and a bowl of water. That old school method would suffice as a quick wash, but with all the intricate parts, moving mechanicals, nooks and crannies, a thorough wash was a full on deep clean.

It's true, the more you look after you bike, the more it will look after you. A deep clean involved using degreaser for the chain, soapy water for the frame, a cloth for the brakes, an old toothbrush for the tight spots, finishing spray for when you're done and some dry or wet lube reapplied to the chain. Washing your bike can take as long as you want it too. Ideally it's best to wash your bike after a cycle; it's done and will be looking brand new for the next ride. Ideal in theory, but in practice I quickly learnt that if I was tired, there was no way I was removing wheels and getting covered in suds. Something I'd chastise myself about when the bike was pulled out for the next ride.

Another lesson I was learning on the bike was etiquette. To wave or not to wave at passing cyclists is and still is an area of cycling that baffles me. I'm not talking a full on wave that jiggles your bingo wings, more so a raise of the hand from the handlebars, or even a friendly nod. I must admit, I love it, it gives me a sense of community and togetherness. Of course cyclists don't *have* to engage in a pleasant exchange, but it is one of those things you either do or don't do. There's also not much you can or really would do if a passerby ignores all friendly gestures. That happens, and you soon forget about it.

I feel the rule is be nice and don't be a dick, and that is interpreted differently. My wave or nod conundrum comes down to where I am and who makes the first move. If I am somewhere remote, or it's early in the morning and I haven't seen any other cyclist for a while, they get a full lift of the hand and good morning. If I'm local, in the city and I expect to see plenty of cyclists I tend to not make the first move, but if I do it's a mere lift of the fingers. If of course a nod or wave came my way first, I'd happily return the gesture. Cycling friends.

There is an exception to this rule, and that's cyclists in a group. What I find is that for some reason, groups of cyclists tend not to wave or nod. Especially if they are wearing full replica kits resembling a professional peloton on a tour. Maybe they all feel that someone else in the group will, and it turns out none of them do. Ay, what can you do?

Lessons coming in thick and fast, cycling in a group is a different ball game altogether. A few friends in my extended network were also getting into cycling and planned to get on board with the approaching Velothon. After knocking up a quick Watsapp group and filling it with cycling banter, we decided to ride the event as a team. Thinking there was nothing more to it than turning up, it was suggested we *practice* cycling as part of a group beforehand. The collective noun for a group of cyclists is a peloton; we resembled a flock of seagulls.

The first practice ride was a steep learning curve, with varying abilities, fitness levels and a range of comfortable speeds meant that you're either too slow or too fast. The idea to work as a unit and take turns at the front seemed pointless, until I was at the back of the pack with reduced drag and happily coasting along the open road, then it made sense. Hand signaling, road calls and riding styles were learnt on the job, but after a few hours we were synchronised and had an idea of who would be the one pulling us around the 85 miles of the Welsh countryside, and it certainly wasn't me. Back home we were all checking our metrics to see how our efforts compared because "If it's not on Strava, it didn't happen".

This is a tongue in cheek poke at someone who claims to have logged any sort of physical activity but doesn't have the "proof" to back it up. Strava is both a blessing and a curse when it comes to logging exercise. Back in 2016 Strava was climbing the ranks and now with almost 100 million users worldwide it is one of the most popular tracking apps out there. Strava soon becomes a ritual after every logged activity, either your phone has logged your run/cycle directly or you have managed to sync it via a smart watch. In these early days my activities were recorded directly to my phone, which in retrospect removed the fear of a failed upload.

With my new found mode of transport exploring new roads, lanes and cycle paths, looking at my Strava account added an extra element into fitness. Not that I was situated anywhere near the top of the leader boards, it was exciting to see how I fared on a particular stretch of road compared to my previous attempt, against myself and competitively against my friends. Obsession kicks in pretty soon when you push extra hard knowing when a segment is coming up on a road ahead.

I was cycling more, still running, getting faster and fitter. On land I was comfortable, with my first event of the "Trilogy" fast approaching, I felt any cycling efforts were converted into stamina which put me in a great position when it came to running the half marathon. Put me in water, and I'm a threat to my very own existence. I needed to get back into that pool and find my balls!

Finding my balls was exactly how my swimming restarted, and it was finding them very exposed when squeezing into what I thought were incorrectly sized swimming shorts. Due to a minor body complex issue I convinced myself out of buying a pair of *speedos* and opted to replace my Aloha surf shorts for a pair of jammers. (I'm guessing they are called jammers as you jam everything into them). Fortunately for my ego, the leisure centre that I attended was frequently occupied by swimming clubs and individuals who knew what they were doing, and were all wearing similarly exposing swimwear.

The overriding take away from my last death defying pool escapade was that I am no way ready for the Olympic sized 50m pool just yet. With a depth of 2 metres there was too much that could go wrong. I needed to earn my stripes in the leisure pool.

The leisure pool is 25m of warm water surrounded by a number of water cannons, colorful slides, fountains and a lazy river. There were no sectioned lanes in this pool, there were no swim start blocks, no swimming clubs carrying out drills and I could stand up with my nipples above the water. It was relatively quiet, and with no children allowed to swim before 10:00 it was only occupied by a small number of elderly folk, who after time became the best cheerleaders a beginner could ask for.

With my hair folded into a swimming cap made for smaller heads and goggles on upside down I was ready to swim. The aim was to restore some pride and make it across without stopping, coughing or drowning. It sure wasn't pretty but I made it, with arms swinging out of sync and legs kicking out of time I was holding my breath with irregular gasps of air. The lifeguard this time on standby, I finally grabbed the opposite side of the pool a victor. Out of breath and in need of a rest, I had time to watch the other swimmers glide through the water length after length, not necessarily fast, but controlled and graceful. There was a technique to swimming, a number of moving parts that when operated at the right time was like poetry in motion. If you miss time the pull of an arm, the turning of your head or the kick of your feet, your body wastes momentum trying to correct the mistake. I was a long way off from getting this technique nailed, but learning how to *breathe out* underwater was my first poolside lesson. I must have looked like an idiot, but the next 20 minutes were spent getting comfortable with the sensation of inhaling air with my face near the water and then exhaling with it just under. The repetition of this, in a safe environment, allowed for my brain to accept this experience and label it as "non life threatening". With this in mind and my "session" coming to an end, I attempt to swim another length. It wasn't as refined as I was expecting, but with each arm stretch and turned head it was all starting to click. It was a mini win in the swim bag. Smelling of chlorine I made my way to work and battled to stay alert in between eating every snack in sight. Swimming is tiring stuff and hungry work!

The Trilogy

Having banked a few successful cycles and chipped away at the swimming, my attention diverted towards running. It was the beginning of March and I had a half marathon to run in a matter of weeks. Oh and not just any half marathon, this was the IAAF Cardiff University World Half Marathon, with all the big dogs taking part.

Typically, when your home town is showcased on TV for a world athletic event, the weather is appalling and it rains sideways all afternoon! Credit to the organisers, volunteers and cheering crowds for sticking it out to support loved ones around the course, the show can't go ahead without those guys. Kudos to the winner Geoffrey Mamworor of Kenya, who after slipping on the timing map at the beginning, managed to beat the crowd favorite Sir Mo Farah. Other than the biblical rain trying to dampen spirits my race went without any incident and I didn't finish too far behind Sir Mo, he crossed the finish line just short of an hour before me. Good one Mo, maybe next time.

The aim of this event was to kick start the three events lined up in aid of Head Start 4 Babies. By now the sponsorship money was coming in and with every donation made, it was converted into motivation. I couldn't and wouldn't back out now; I was too determined to see this through. Even though at this stage running was my stronger discipline, I purposely added the pressure of aiming for a personal best of a sub 2 hour finish. By sticking with the 2 hour pace maker in the pen ahead of me, I was relatively safe in the knowledge that when I crossed that wet finish line my first goal was complete.

That afternoon, in my finishers' t-shirt and medal, I sat with my feet up, a milky brew in one hand, and in the other my phone, scrolling through my Strava stats counting the kudos awarded by fellow followers.

Half marathon ticked off, two more challenges left, although technically the triathlon is three challenges in itself, so FOUR challenges left! It was time to address one of the biggest elephants in the room - open water swimming. I was swimming in the leisure pool with Stella, Linda, Graham and Paul most mornings but I could barely string 200m together without stopping. I was convinced the cycling and running would assist my overall endurance, but the rhythm and timing in the water were proving difficult to master. Doubt was starting to creep into my mind and I was getting frustrated with the evident lack of progress. I also had to address the small matter of not only reaching the goal of 750m in a pool, but also clocking that distance in some open water in preparation for race day. Living on the coast meant that the sea was the most obvious choice to dip my toe in. Barry Island was about 8 miles away, right next to where I work and free admission. So of course I decided that heading to a disused quarry, 35 miles away, with the maximum depth of 75m was the best thing for me to do.

The rationale behind this decision was based solely on the fact that my first triathlon would be swum in the supposedly calm and supposedly fresh water of Cardiff Bay. In my clearly amateur I-don't-know-what-I'm-doing mind I figured gaining open water exposure in the sea would be futile as I read somewhere that your body acts differently in salt water compared to fresh water. In a way this was right, but this slight nuance bore insignificant when it came to swimming in the open. Open water swimming is open water swimming, it all helps.

Before I met the challenges of open water swimming, I realised that I actually needed a wetsuit. My research process starts on a well-known, online only sports store. I search wetsuits, filter by price, sort low to high, and I go from there. There was very little deliberation – I needed a wetsuit, and after a crash course in neoprene and measuring body parts with an IKEA tape measure, an entry level Orca wetsuit would do. It arrived within the week, unexpectedly with a pair of white gloves to wear while putting on the suit. They were to help prevent snagging the whale like rubber while squeezing in each time. They proved a massive faff and ended up being worn only once.

Next hurdle was testing the suit in a controlled environment that was not a disused filled quarry, that meant I was off to the pool. Have you ever seen someone wearing a wetsuit in a swimming pool? Well fortunately for me I had a few weeks before, so I at least thought this was normal. The leisure pool would have been a bit too toasty, so I waved goodbye to the swimming crew and tiptoed sheepishly to the big boy pool. Walking to that Olympic size swimming pool brought back a whole host of memories, and I was now wearing a wetsuit! Standing out like a sore thumb I ignored both the wide eyed stares, bypassed the steps, and got on with it, jumped straight in, no faffing. My immediate thought, other than instantly needing a wee, was that the overall feeling was lovely. I was bobbing around, treading water without spending too much energy if at all, and it felt great.

Fortunately by now my swimming had improved and I could now comfortably swim a full 50m without drinking half the pool. I completed my first full length in record timing, the neoprene doing exactly what the description stated. It kept my hips high and my shoulders flexible. I was flying! I was still a long way from my goal of 15 lengths (750m) but I still had a bit of time to get there.

The following week I was over to the insanely deep quarry for some open water survival, with a wetsuit, swimming cap, goggles and bag full of confidence. That bag was soon emptied when I saw the size of the quarry. It was enormous, but I had come too far to back out now. I paid my money, signed away my life, and jumped into a minibus full of scuba divers down to the jetty. The short trip down to the water was all a little surreal, I was already way out of my depth and I was still in the bus having nervous conversations with scuba Steve and his buddies. The further into the quarry the bus drove, the higher the surrounding walls became. This wasn't a good idea, I already knew this experience would be over soon.

Everything I had "learnt" in the pool over the last few months went straight out of the window the moment I pushed off from the jetty. The temperature of the water was minus Moscow, my hands and feet froze and my bollocks recoiled in fear. My heart pounded through my wetsuit and panic hit when it dawned on me that I couldn't touch the bottom, let alone see it. What the fuck was I doing!? I managed a shit 20 minutes of questionable breast stroke and intermittent front crawl before calling it a day. The water was far too cold to get my face in for a stretch of anything that resembled someone training for a triathlon, my breathing and heart rate was so erratic I think I may have been close to a panic attack. I soon got out, dried, got back to the minibus, up out of the quarry and straight back into the car. I was inconsolable. I numbed the waves of doubt by scoffing a packet of four chocolate bars on the way home. The whole trip was a colossal failure, I needed help and maybe more time.

Before any of that there were 86 miles (140km) of cycling up next, and thankfully I had some friends who would join me for the ride. This was my biggest event in terms of duration, distance and danger. A lot could go wrong on the bike so this was making me a bit nervy. You could have a crash, someone could crash into you, your bike could develop a mechanical or you could bonk, and bonking wasn't as good as it may sound.

Prior to this event and in between my swimming antics, I had managed to *recce* a few of the climbs, so other than the amount of time spent in the saddle, I kind of knew what to expect, and knowing what's to come is sometimes half the battle.

The Tumble, found on the outskirts of Abergavenny is a beautiful 3.1 mile (5km) long climb running parallel to a beautiful Welsh Valley; it averages at 8% gradient and maxes out at 15%. Negotiate the switch back hair pin, the cattle grid and sheep and you're up the top in less than 30 minutes on a good day.

This climb is about 35 miles from Cardiff so instead of burning too much energy I happily took a few car trips up to Abergavenny and cycled the climb on fresh legs. Cheating? Nah, in terms of preparation for this climb, it was needs must. Caerphilly Mountain on the other hand was closer to home so I was able to get a decent warm up before getting to Caerphilly.

Caerphilly Mountain is a relatively short, sharp climb in comparison to The Tumble. At 0.8 miles (1.4km) long, with an average gradient of 9.2% and peaking at a maximum of 18.7% it's a different kettle of fish. You approach the beginning as you head out of the town and it takes a while for your eyes to adjust to what's in front of you. With trees lined either side it gives the illusion that you're cycling towards a wall. Twisting up and out of sight, additional bends and false summits, it separates the men from the boys, and after 5 hours of cycling it really is a case of seeing what is left in the tank come event day.

The Velothon kicks off in waves and the "Cyclopaths" (our genius team name) set off according to our forecasted finish time of around 6 to 7 hours. We needed to maintain an average speed of 15 mph or more to avoid being picked up by the sweeper vehicle. The pro cyclists were taking to the course shortly after us and we needed to be out of their way beforehand.

With closed roads, dry weather and adrenaline coursing through our bodies we set off at a brisk pace. The first 25 miles were flat and fast, this meant any strategy of conserving energy for the hills was lost early on. We were out of Cardiff, through Newport and storming towards the picturesque, quaint village of Usk within about three hours. This is where the first food stop was situated. The feed stations consisted of bananas, crisps, energy gels, water, hydration tablets and already tired cyclists. With our legs rested for a few minutes we stocked up on essentials and got moving knowing the next station was the other side of the Tumble.

By the time we weaved through lanes and villages, avoiding crashes and mechanicals we hit the almighty Tumble. Up until this moment the team stayed in close proximity, but now it was a case of survival of the fittest and "I'll see you up the top mate" bravado. It is all well and good having done your reconnaissance mission in the weeks prior, but on fresh legs it proved pointless. After 56 miles clocked, nearing the most I had ever cycled, the climbing of this hill was testing a lot of people, including myself. Lactic acid build up, cramp, upset stomach and dehydration was turning some cyclists into walkers, and there was nothing wrong with that. We had all signed up for a day out on the bike, but no one here was a pro cyclist. However, stopping or walking just wasn't an option for me, so I dropped into my easiest gear and proceeded to grind it out. I was getting up that hill in one piece and I would use all the curse words in my repository to do so.

In these circumstances I found digging deep came naturally to me. I can take the pain, exhaustion and every call of my body telling me to stop, and convert it into determination. I can take myself away from the situation I've put myself in and I can take my mind to happy thoughts. That day the thoughts that circled my brain included the people who supported me during my challenge, the money that had been donated, the babies who will be helped, my friends and my family. This was working, I would take my mind to a happy place, and then when that ran dry I could switch my brain to a dark place and think of any wrongs I've endured, any heartache, frustration and buried anger. I was able to use the negativity and just…keep…moving…forward. Not sure if that's healthy and I should probably speak to someone about that, but the mind is ever so powerful and it makes the difference when the tough gets going.

…and then I reached the summit, happy days. The gang reconvenes at the top for a little rest, an extension of the legs and a catch of breath. We take on some hydration and a sneaky sausage roll as a reward. We then set off again knowing what goes up must come down. The descent to the second food station is a long stretch of smooth tarmac road that was easy to navigate and it was just what was needed, a perfect time to bag some free miles and only move the legs to keep them warm.

20 miles later, after crossing a few valleys, battling wind in all directions and fatigue knocking at the door, Caerphilly wall turns up and I'm back in my happy, dark, angry place again. The main difference this time around is that you have the

locals lining the road with motivational words etched on banners, families cheering, groups shouting and all verbally pushing you up the last big climb of the day. The support around the majority of the route is impressive. The smaller villages, with their roads closed off, struggle to do much else other than get involved. The crowds at Caerphilly were more helpful than they would ever know. No stopping, no walking – I was getting up that mountain if it was the last thing I did. And I bloody well did. By now all the salts, sugars, energy gels and sausage rolls are playing fun and games in my stomach and the only goal, with 8 miles until the finish line, was to not shit myself. Looking around I took some relief in knowing that we all felt the same.

Velothon Wales was a great day out on the bike and it's a huge shame that it could no longer continue after 2018. The Cyclopaths avoided injury, mechanicals, any dreaded bonks and crossed the line after about 7 hours of cycling. We were all pretty broken so scooted off to the pub and toasted to our conquest to share our stories. For me, I toasted to another challenge of mine completed, the Velothon was in the bag. The Cardiff triathlon was next up; I just had to cycle home first.

Two down and one to go, but the Cardiff Triathlon was the big one, my El Captain. Based on my swimming technique, it was the event where I could actually die, or at least get dragged out of the water by the support crew on a kayak. I needed some sort of contingency plan to survive this triathlon, and without any shame I figured all I needed to do was get out of the water within 60 minutes, that was the cut off time before the human fishing commenced and my race would be deemed a DNF. I had already proved I am willing to fight to the finish line, and I just needed to get on with it.

The last pieces to the triathlon puzzle included the purchase of a tribelt, to pin my race number to, and a very revealing trisuit. Not that this lanky 6ft frame had anything to show, it's just the trisuit really didn't leave much to the imagination. Testing out the trisuit meant my neighbourhood had an eyeful during a test run around the block, but I was beyond caring, it was a piece of the triathlon puzzle that was needed. Wetsuit back on, trisuit on underneath and into the pool I go for a full dress rehearsal and some more character building. After 30 minutes and 17 seconds I finished executing the objective, and that was to swim 750m without stopping. By swim I mean move through the water in a forward motion, and by swim I don't necessarily mean front crawl. There were all sorts of survival methods being used to clock the distance and break down this mental barrier I had erected. It started positively with front crawl but soon mutated into breast stroke which at times evolved into good old fashion doggy paddle. I didn't care, I just needed to keep moving and not cling on to the side to have a breather. My "swimming" must have brought some humor to the lifeguards, probably half thinking they would have to put their life saving training to the test. Stand down boys; I made it without the need of the kiss of life.

In other news, the trisuit also passed the test, bonus! With the general costs of these challenges adding up I was looking to save a bit of cash and decided on an unknown brand of trisuit from an online megastore. The padding in the shorts did provide the sensation of swimming with a nappy on but it was all bearable.

The last week of "training" was kept light for no reason other than I was exhausted. I still couldn't swim, there was a list of rules I had to remember and I was generally bricking it. There was however a whole load of support behind me and other than letting them down, at least I was there, at the start line ready to see what the hell would happen when I entered my first triathlon. The unknown could lead to some glorious triathlon adventures or haunt me for years to come.

I heard that nobody sleeps the night before their first triathlon and for me that was true. You force feed a carbohydrate loaded evening meal and spend far too much energy trying to put all the race numbers on your gear perfectly. With my wave kicking off before 07:00 I needed to be in, set up and out of the transition zone before stupid o'clock. This also meant waking up early, to stomach some sort of fuel to get me to the start line, but not too much that I needed a toilet stop mid way through the cycle. With all sorts of negative outcomes whirling through my head it was no wonder I didn't sleep well.

One sobering moment during the racking of my bike in the transition area the next day was that some people take this sport seriously. The bikes, the helmets, the shoes and just the general focus of these amateurs was admirable. At no point did I ever think I would finish this race anywhere noteworthy, but it was laughable to say that I would be competitive in comparison.

Comparison is the thief of joy, and I wanted to enjoy this experience whether it was my first or last. I hung my bike and laid out my running shoes, bike shoes, a towel, socks and pinned my race number to my tri belt. I also kept an Asthma inhaler in my bag and as a safety blanket I decided to squeeze an inhaler up the sleeve of my wetsuit. Although my Asthma is under control, I very rarely exercise without one nearby. There were also drink bottles and energy gels to hand. I made some mental notes as to where this was all situated in a spread of 100's of other looking transition setups and then found a toilet to release some last minute nerves. I was ready (ish).

After composing myself, I applied my race tattoos on upside-down and made my way over to the holding pen full of nervous triathletes which amusingly I found some were wearing the same wetsuit as me. There were a number of first timers here, and after some fleeting conversations I realised I wasn't alone. A lot of individuals, wearing the same entry level orca wetsuit, were all giving triathlon a go for the first time. With a strange sort of camaraderie and togetherness we made our way to the water when our start time was nearing. The race director bellows some health and safety rules and explains the swim route, it's a two right hand sided turn, out and back loop. Seems an obvious statement to make, but at the time I thought "Shit, 750m looks a hell of a lot further in open water than 15 lengths of a 50m pool".

I walked slowly down to the jetty, strategically positioning myself at the back of the pack, out of everyone else's way. We jumped into the cold, brown, murky but fresh water of Cardiff Bay and tread water for far too long, regulating our body and wetsuit temperature with energy sapping away every second, it was go time. Goggles on, the countdown begins and we ready ourselves.

The klaxon echoes around the Bay and off we go, my arms spinning, my legs kicking and my heart rate pounding like sonar to the mysteries below. Two things occur at the early stages that I realised practicing beforehand would have been a good idea. Sighting, that's when after every few revolutions of the arms you stick you head up to check you're heading in the right direction. There was none of that. Bi-lateral breathing, when you're able to breathe either side of your swim stroke for multiple advantages, there was none of that either. Doggy paddle, panicking and a new one for the event, backstroke! I alternated those techniques for the majority of the start, but it was working. What I didn't factor into my slow and steady pace was the second wave of swimmers starting 5 minutes after me.

The comfort zone of being at the back of the pack meant that I didn't have to worry about anyone behind me, but that only lasted for about 10 minutes as the speedy swimmers of the following wave were gunning for me, and I could see them, because I was on my back. Things got interesting at this point, more panic set in and more water was swallowed. I could see the finish line but I was on the longest stretch of the swim, energy was depleting and I was just staying afloat, moving forward, slowly. Kayakers on standby.

If I had a stronger discipline, and it's clear by now that it's not swimming. My never say die attitude was stronger and as I neared dry land I could see and hear the supporters, it was a Godsend. After zigzagging for far too long I had to keep my forward motion in a straight line. Without being able to pinpoint exactly who was shouting, and to who, I imagined it was my friends and family cheering me on. I find some energy and kick so much that I get a cramp in my foot. Hampered slightly I keep kicking and hit the exit ramp, before I know it I'm being assisted up and out of the water. The swim was over and the realisation of being on terra firma resulted in a release of my own cheering, but more like a war cry of a Viking who had just conquered an old foe. I swore I would never do that again, telling anyone who would hear it.

It wasn't over, I still had the cycle and run to get through with the transitions in between. I was out of the water but not out of the wetsuit, that took a lot of effort to take off. I wiggled out of the top half during my walk to the bike which took longer as I struggled to remember where my bike actually was. Checking the bike rack numbers I finally found my area. I dry my feet, slip off the rest of my wetsuit, dry my feet again and put on some wet socks. I was such a novice, but there is a smile on my face as I'm being heckled by my friends on the sideline.

Transition one was slow and after trundling out of the transition zone I climbed aboard the noble stead and set off on three loops of some flat and beautifully smooth tarmac. Pace is steadily increasing with each lap and I'm successfully overtaking other riders, but it's difficult to know if I am making any real progress or just catching up to the waves that overtook me during the swim. Knowing I will need an energy boost on the run I consume some energy gels and a cereal bar for some sugar spikes, it should see me to the end. The three loops came to an end and having seen friends and family on multiple occasions I was ready to finish strong.

Transition two was a lot quicker than the first as there was less to do, take off your helmet, change over your shoes and switch the race number around from the back to the front, easy with a tribelt. All that lay ahead was a 5k run, my strongest leg. I had run countless 5k's so in my mind it was like a parkrun, an out and back flat run over the barrage which I had run 100's of times before. I was confident, I was doing this, just don't fuck it up. I use my straight-out-of-the-box, go to, tried and tested motivational booster – the crowd. Channeling the cheers and words of encouragement is a great way to forget the pain and fatigue. They may not know you, but they want you to succeed and finish as much as you do. I show my gratitude and thanks, hoping that my efforts are inspiring just one of the supporters. It is a massive kick up the backside during the last few minutes of the event.

The last 500m of the run course banks around the Wales Millennium Centre where understandably there are no crowds as they are at the finish line waiting for you to reappear. During those last few quiet strides I was allowed to take it all in and spend a few moments with my thoughts, acknowledging the commitment to the unknown, the physical training I had put in just to get to the start line. For me the biggest reward was the money raised and support from friends and loved ones. Filled with relief, pride and a last shot of adrenaline, I scrape the bottom of the energy barrel and hit the last corner in a full on sprint down the carpet to applause and cheers.

I cross the line with a release of just sheer joy, shouting and making a racket. I wanted everyone to see that although I couldn't really swim, that I got lost in the transition area, that the bike was a bit pedestrian and the run was a plod, I still made it around my first triathlon and I was living proof that it was achievable. Crossing that line I became a triathlete. I collect my medal and placed it around my neck for the rest of the day. The official results come via text message shortly which outlined a breakdown of the three disciplines and my total time. To my surprise the swim time was 20 minutes! All that panicking must have made me swim faster than I originally thought was possible. The bike took just under 40 minutes and the run a disappointing 28 minutes, but I was generally chuffed with my performance overall.

William's Warriors

The triathlon dust had barely settled and an email finds its way to my inbox, CARDIFF TRIATHLON 2017 EARLY BIRD OFFER! I sign up, without hesitation. Not only was I now well and truly bitten by the triathlon bug, but I set a benchmark and I wanted to better myself. I would have another year of swimming under my belt, more time on the bike and would have pounded the pavement a whole lot more. The Cardiff Triathlon is my home town race and I'm unable to see how I couldn't be involved in some way, shape or form. Another factor secured my registration, the fact that I had inspired a few friends to get involved too; they must have thought they could do better! Either way, there was now some healthy competition in the mix which added extra spice to training. The heartwarming feeling overall was that I was now part of a small group of people working towards the same goal.

Speaking of goals, with no other events, half marathons or challenges lined up for the rest of 2016 the New Year swings by quickly with an off season lasting a little longer than planned. Unfortunately, when restarting the training I found myself a bit further back in terms of fitness and ability than I would have liked to be.

Although the running does continue at a leisurely pace, the swimming takes a while to get back into and with no indoor bike set up the winter tends to write off any progressive cycling. Still, I knew what to expect in the summer of 2017, so I take that complacency and stupidly side with cockiness when talking to the new triathlon recruits. It's reminiscent of back in school when you and your friends claim not to have done much studying, only for the exam to come around and they ace it, while you're left wondering what went wrong. I was heading towards that scenario but obviously enjoying the questions, dishing out advice and loving the attention, I was happy reliving my first triathlon to anyone prepared to listen.

Cycling to work during the wet, cold and dark winter months was hardly appealing, so my morning routine mainly involved time spent ticking over in the pool to build my swim form and dubious technique mixed with frequent visits to the gym to take part in high intensity group workout sessions. The class sessions included multiple stations of equipment that resembled torture devices which soon became surrounded with droplets of sweat, and maybe even tears. A typical round would start on the speed mill, then on to the rower, then abdominal crunches, followed by battle ropes, alternative lunges, assisted pull ups, kettle bell swings and dumbbell lifts. 1 minute on, 30 seconds rest in between. It was grueling, but I convinced it was effective for the multi-disciples of triathlon, and it also injected a source of companionship during training. It wasn't long until there was a core group of recurring attendees putting ourselves through the high intensity onslaught. There was camaraderie in shared pain.

On the rare occasions of a dry spell and to mix it up when possible, I would pop on the warmer leggings and waterproof jacket (just in case) and take the opportunity to the leave the car at home and cycle the 8 miles to work.

One occasion comes to mind, and for the reason that something happened for the very first time is why I'll never forget it. With plenty of layers on and clothes prepped already awaiting me in the office, I set out early to beat any build up of traffic. Taking in a loop of Cardiff Bay I soon realise that with a chill in the air, the roads are occasionally laid with a ground frost. The sensible and rational part of my brain would operate common sense and turned back to avoid any difficulty. The carefree, adventurous, lets-see-what-happens side of my brain pushed on making shapes in the air with my breath.

What happens when you take an icy corner at speed, the obvious! Veering left my front wheel hits a patch of black ice and my bike slips from underneath me heading towards the right. With both feet snapping out of the pedals, I continue to hit the ground in the forward motion I was travelling.

With a grazed knee, grazed elbow, a sore shoulder and a bruised ego I lay still internally assessing if there was any other damage I should be concerned about. Confirming I wasn't dead, I picked myself up and gingerly trotted over to the bike which to my surprise and maybe because of the ice, only suffered a slight shredded handlebar and a dink to the frame.

Onlookers checked if I was ok, and by now, knowing I was alright, seeing the smile on my face they were satisfied in letting me cycle, very slowly to work.

Upon showering at my destination and with the adrenaline worn off, it's now apparent that I must have hit the ground pretty hard, as the side of my bottom is now different colour to the rest of my body. They are only superficial; the lasting concern was the graze on my helmet. This was only checked once I had removed it once arriving at the office and after seeing the scuff mark I understood the importance of this assuming piece of kit. I may have been in a bit of a pickle had I not been wearing one, granted I was playing with fire cycling on ice, I'll still always wear one.

Winter subsides, and with spring brings group rides and the temptation of more open water swimming. As a group we practice "brick" sessions, where two disciplines are carried out in quick succession. If I learnt anything from my debut it was to get a move on during the transitions. The open water swimming became more accessible as the Cardiff International White Water centre opened up their training area for swimmers. This allowed a near 200m loop of swimming in a controlled and safe environment. Perfect for open water exposure, to practice sighting and to get some use out of the wetsuit. I was also acting as someone to lean on during the newbie's introduction to all things triathlon. My guidance was always based on experience and not necessarily knowledge. To be honest, I still didn't really have a clue.

My second attempt of the Velothon Wales once again went without any concerns. The route remained the same, so did the torture of the two previously aforementioned climbs. This time around I had the assurance and lived experience of getting up them without stopping or walking. That was enough. With a few curse words thrown into the mix I had no issues. The extra year cycling was noticeable, I was stronger, more comfortable and I knew what I was doing. So it was another good day out followed by a beer and far too much flatulence after all the gels and sugary drinks consumed.

Almost a month later I was standing in the holding pen, getting psyched for my second Cardiff sprint triathlon, but this time with added competition. Typically one friend used to swim for Wales as a youngster and was also the person who got me into cycling, Thomas. Another friend called Ron was in the Royal Navy and was naturally fit and strong. Experience was all I had, so I lowered my expectations to finish faster than them, and aimed to finish faster than my previous outing.

Turns out I don't perform well under pressure and heightened expectation. An unforeseen panic during the swim prompted more breast stroke than I wanted, but even with no backstroke and doggy paddling I finished the swim 6 minutes slower the previous year. Although feeling stronger on the bike I finished slower but only by a few seconds. It was also during this leg that I was overtaken by my friend who started in the wave after me, ego dented I pushed on. The run was my saving grace on the day, shaving 3 minutes from my previous year.

In no way was this a race between friends, but naturally when you're pitted and compared against your closest buddies you want to be seen towards the top of whatever it is you're doing. That's normal; we are all human, that's how we work. But sitting in the pub, with our medals on, laughing about the choppy swim, the hair pin corners, encouraging each other on the run and cheering others across the finish line, we encapsulated, right there, what triathlon was all about. That camaraderie, the comradeship and togetherness we all shared that morning would be the overwhelming last line. We finished our drinks and bought some more.

The next few days I tried to deconstruct what went wrong during what should have been a quicker triathlon. But nothing went wrong. I panicked in the swim, I set out too quickly on the bike trying to make up lost ground on the swim and could have paced the run even better, but nothing went *wrong*. It was a learning curve and I was bagging valuable experience that I was determined to take to other events. I was still deep in the triathlon fold, I wanted more and once again, when the early bird email dropped into my inbox, I signed up straight away. This time however the plan was to up the ante and get an Olympic distance triathlon under my tribelt.

In terms of events, that was it for 2017. A quiet year in comparison but with having a trip to Vancouver that summer I simply didn't have enough money to enter any more races. In retrospect my body may have been preparing me for what life was about to throw its way. 2018 would be the year I pushed the limits further than a lot of people thought was safe.

This was because 2017 ended in a somber mood as tragically a friend of mine passed away which totally rocked our foundations. He was taken far too soon to the cruel hands of cancer. It was both the saddest time of close friends and family, but also the catalyst that spurred so much love, support and recognition in the name of our friend. William was infamously kind, charming and pretty much the best man you could ever meet. When he was diagnosed with cancer he was referred to Velindre Cancer Centre in Cardiff. At the darkest of times it was a fantastic place that offered advice, support and most importantly the treatment he desperately needed.

The hospital treats over 1.5 million patients every year, and continues to put a huge focus on research and clinical trials. The staff were pretty incredible too and were always there for him.

In thanks to this support, a large number of friends and family grouped together to start over a year of fundraising events, races and stupendous challenges spanning Ireland to Luxembourg with donations to the cancer centre coming in from all parts of the world.

2018 was in honor of William, and we raised a grand total £21,510 in his name.

The year of fundraising kicked off with a 10k Obstacle course race in March, in a place called Merthyr Mawr, famous for its Big Dipper sand dunes.

This was my first event raising money in my friend's name and I was pumped for it. Strangely, for the first time ever, I was actually in the best shape I had ever been in. The weeks spanning Christmas and New Years were normally hijacked by gluttony and I'd fill my face with beer and chocolate. That was still the case, but those days were counterbalanced by continual trips to the gym and swimming pool. This may have been a grieving coping strategy but it worked wonders with my general health and well being.

The klaxon sounds and the smoke from the cannons gets right up in your lungs, I'm off on a 10k run full of mud, sands and seasonably cold water. Obstacles were pretty standard, they included climbing over shit, ducking under shit and quite literally crawling through shit. Running on my own meant I was able to pace the 10k to my liking and after negotiating a number of obstacles I found myself in unknown territory, at the front of the pack.

My surprisingly unusual position didn't last too long, the big dipper rendered its ugly head and it was making a meal out of the others. After giving the sandy incline a powerful run up, my strength was soon ousted. Incapable of maintaining a steady cadence and I was overtaken by a trio of young lads who were seemingly out for just a laugh. Credit to my fitness I was able to keep them in sight so I managed to hold some dignity. Running on sand is tough; running *up* sand is painful. It is great fun but it also gets everywhere, and I do mean EVERYWHERE! Wearing a custom printed t-shirt with the charity details was a constant reminder of the reason for putting myself through this self inflicted ordeal. I crossed the muddy finish line just behind the lads, proud of my performance and happy to tick off my first of many events in 2018, but I was still finding sand in parts of my body for days afterwards.

Race for Victory was up next, this is a 5k closed road route around the town where William lived in Cardiff, and also where he received his cancer treatment. It was a smaller event and numbers were limited, but a number of friends decided to sign up and there was no way I was missing this one. It took place on Sunday the 5th May, it was a bank holiday weekend and it was a hot one! You know those runs when it's just too hot to run without adequately hydrating? Yep, it was one of those runs. No PB's were even attempted that day, with piss poor planning it was just a case of enjoying the run on an emotional occasion. The finishing times were all soon forgotten after a few beers and a sing song in the local pub.

June swings around and I'm gearing up for a new triathlon event. The inaugural *All or Nothing –* SWYD triathlon taking place at Barry Island. SWYD is an acronym for Sleep When You're Dead, not a Welsh word pronounced *swede* (like some people thought it was). This event was another sprint distance triathlon, but this time it was a sea swim. Oh and not just any sea swim, this swim was in the Bristol Channel, the second highest tidal range in the world, only exceeded by the Bay of Fundy in Canada. What does that mean in swimming terms? It means that when the tide changes, it changes fast. It means you could be swimming one way in at record speeds, but swim the other direction and you'll hardly move.

With dangerous rip tides and unpredictable currents it's a tricky slice of coast to navigate. The organisers were well aware of the dangers and ensured the tide was just right for an out, across and back 750m route.

My training had continued well enough prior to this event with running and cycling kept to a level of just maintaining momentum. I wasn't setting any training targets to hit, if anything I was making it all up as I was going along. Training with no real direction proves very laborious and boring. I was however making major progress in the pool. After speaking to a swimmer who used the leisure pool as a warm down, she convinced me to give the weekly triathlon swim sessions a go. After making excuses for a few weeks, I couldn't hide much longer, and after further nagging I found myself with the daunting prospect of embarrassing myself in front of swimmers training for an Ironman.

Meeting James that Wednesday morning was a turning point. Feeling totally exposed in my jammers with 50m of pool in front of me might have been one of those indirect life saving moments. James was a seasoned triathlete, strength and conditioning coach and multiple Ironman finisher. He knew what he was talking about and had the qualifications to back it. I was in safe hands. I told him what I wanted to achieve, to complete the Olympic distance triathlon, to which out loud he said "OK, let's go", but inside he questioned, "is that all?"

What he had planned for me was more than what I even thought was possible.

Swimming with a group, with instructions, pointers on techniques, drills and endurance sets was all new to me. Having someone to push you constantly, even when you feel you have no more to give, was encouraging beyond words. It wasn't easy, it wasn't pretty, but it was effective and proved the missing element for me. Confidence was building, and when only after a few months of these sessions I was able to keep up with the rest of the group, I could actually see progress. I was genuinely enjoying the swimming because even though it doesn't get easier, you are able to do more. The mixed incorporation of pull buoys, hand paddles and flippers added a whole new level of excitement. Come my first triathlon of the year, my swimming was noticeably different, no more backstroke and doggy paddling for me.

Registration complete, bike racked in the transition area and the head squeezed into a really tight swimming cap, I was ready for the Bristol Channel. The race briefing took place on the promenade and it's at that point you realise the swim exit to the transition area is a fair old dap away.

Other than the typical race rules that now were commonplace to me, the additional causes for concern were sighting the turn buoys. It was hard to see from the promenade but counter intuitively you need to *not* aim directly for the first one, and aim 45 degrees to the left of it as the current will be pulling you right. Aim too straight and you'll end up swimming against the tide just to make the turn. Not everyone heed this advice, and that was clear from the eager beavers who shot off first after the claxon.

Swimming was well and truly a test during that first leg of the race. The salt water provided extra buoyancy, but with the mass start and the addition of slight waves makes for a tactical dog fight just to get through the flailing arms and legs.

Hoot goes the hooter and a few hundred triathlete wannabes run through the sand and into the water. Getting to the waves my heart rate was somewhat doubled compared to a swim start I was used to. Not only was it raised due to the fact I was starting a triathlon, but also because the race started by a brisk run into the water. It's funny watching the people ahead gauging when to stop running and start swimming, there's no right or wrong way to get going. You either start swimming and realise it's too soon as you claw away at the sand below, or you carry on wading as fast as you can until the waves are making it too difficult to move forward any more.

Not forgetting the advice of heading far left, it's a case of battling the swimmers who had different plans. You soon notice the strength of the current when you realise you didn't hang left enough. As soon as I hit the first turn buoy it was like the handbrake was lifted, I was gliding through the water, the rhythm was steady and only broken by an ill timed break of a wave. Riding the waves on the last length of the swim is a joy. With this handbrake fully released you're now rolling downhill.

Just like the entrance to the swim, the end is met with a similarly mixed exit strategy. Some stood and waded when they could touch the sand with their feet, some only stood when they could grab the sand. Not sure if there is any written rule. All I knew was that it was over and I now started the long run back up to the transition area to get sorted for the bike leg.

Unfortunately while exiting the water it was clear that someone was in great difficulty on the shore line. It was sad to see a number of people providing first aid to a fellow swimmer who had been dragged out of the water after experiencing some trouble shortly beforehand.

Not knowing this, myself and a number of other competitors continued on through transition and into the bike, discussing what we had seen and praying they were alright. There was nothing we could do other than push on. With thoughts refocused to the cycle I hit the road out of Barry Island. The bike route was a 20k out and back loop, with a few tasty climbs thrown in for good measure.

The bike went by without any issues, much to the relief of my heightened anxiety. The bike leg was out and back on the same open roads. So at the halfway mark you were 10k away from the finish line. As obvious as that sounds, my fear of having a mechanical or accident so far away from the start/finish line was irrational. It didn't help that the roads remained open during the event. It was relatively early for a Sunday which meant less traffic, but roundabouts, junctions and traffic lights were still operable, and the rules of the road were still to be followed. I can honestly say that the majority, if not all of the riders broke multiple Highway Code offences that morning!

The other mentionable moment that sticks out during this race was that during my fuzzy transition I had forgotten to remove my goggles.

Of course they had been removed from my face, but they had been pulled down to sit around my neck. It was a good 10 minutes into the cycle when the first climb came around that someone, with a massive grin on their face, taking great pleasure from it, told me about the goggles adding unnecessary weight to my bike. It's difficult to take goggles off around your head and helmet without stopping, so I kept them on for the whole cycle.

Having broken a number of road rules, dodged traffic and taken a few late amber traffic lights, the 10k turn point came and I just wanted to get off the bike. A few people hadn't been as lucky and did find themselves waiting for the sweeper bus to take them back, luckily I managed to avoid any concerns, or so I thought.

On the last descent, just prior to the last stretch of causeway heading back onto the island it seems that a misplaced directional marker led a few cyclists down the wrong road. Having seen this from mid way down the descent I could see they were making no attempt to turn around and figured that knowing the roads a little better it may be best to help them out. Catching up and leading them on a little detour we regained the actual route having probably lost 2-3 minutes on the others nearby. We were never in a winning position so it made sense to ensure they didn't get totally lost.

Getting off the bike was a relief but also painful. Lessons in fuel management and salt balances would take a while for me to master and cramp set in almost immediately after the first few footsteps. With the pain unbearable I stop at Marco's Café, made famous by TV's Gavin and Stacey, and stretched my legs before wrapping up a general plod of a 5k run through the island, up and down the causeway, then up over Friars Point and back to finish line under the pavilion.

For so many reasons the first triathlon at Barry island was a memorable one. With no real benchmark set it was a case of getting it done as preparation for the bigger challenge the following month. Swimming was a noticeable improvement, the cycle was steady and the run was paced comfortably after recovering from cramp. Completing the event came with a nice bag full of swag to take home and a nice new medal to cap off a well organised event with plenty of room for improvement.

On a sobering note, the confirmed news filtered through at the finish line that the gentleman pulled out of the water unfortunately suffered cardiac arrest and tragically passed away shortly after paramedics arrived.

There seemed to be a number of tragic incidents during triathlons, half marathons and marathons around that time. Naturally my thoughts go out to the friends and family who have lost a loved one during these or any event. Personally, I know that if anything happened to me during an event, I would want my friends and family to know that I was doing something I loved, fully aware of the risks. Of course no one expects to die during an event and tend not to think twice about signing over insurance waivers and the rest of it. Events do come with a suggestion to seek medical advice before entering, but who really does that unless they know they have, or had an issue? The awareness of available medical screenings to detect underlying issues are more known now, but having spoken to individuals training for events the common consensus tends to be "oh I wouldn't want to get checked out in case the Doctor tells me I shouldn't take part in an event I really want to do". Ignorance is bliss, ay?

Even with that in mind, it was time to ramp up the ante, and with three sprint distance triathlons to my name, it was time to chalk up an Olympic time. The pressure was off, this was me versus me and to even get to the start line was the goal, finishing this event was the bonus. It's funny to say this now, but completing the Olympic distance triathlon in Cardiff would be the top of the goals board for me. Crossing that finish line would be recognition that I completed something I really didn't think was possible. Looking back to the doggy paddling in the pool to swimming 1500m in open water and completing this event was the pinnacle for me. I had nothing else to prove to myself.

Leading up to this event I must admit I was quietly confident in my swimming ability. For the first time I felt like I was actually able to swim without panicking, stressing out or flapping around like a total idiot. This was partly down to the swim sessions I had been attending plus the use of the Cardiff International White Water centre (CIWW).

The CIWW centre is a great place for adrenaline fuelled activities based on the water. Kayaking and canoeing down the man made rapids, or learning to paddle board on the quieter section. This quieter section was open to swimmers every Thursday morning and provided an opportunity to swim a near 200m loop of fresh open water. While it was chemically treated and safe to swim in, it's recommended not to drink too much, and it was the best comparison to swimming in the Bay for the Cardiff triathlon. The centre was also across the road from the Cardiff International Pool as part of the Sports Village; perfectly situated for open water swimming practice.

Most, if not every Thursday morning during the summer was spent in my wetsuit, swimming lap after lap before heading to work. By now, in my third year of taking part in triathlons I was starting to know the faces of the regulars and individuals who are just as keen. What is also apparent now is that I am no longer a total novice, and on occasions I'm providing advice, support and encouragement to others starting off in triathlon. Even though I wasn't competitive in any way, the triathlon community around me was growing and the people I frequently trained alongside and met at events were starting to become friends.

Habits, rituals and traditions now play a big part of my triathlon preparation. Eating a certain pasta dish the night before an event, the early morning porridge and the setting up of the transition area all follow a similar process. If it works, why change it right? Nerves were accepted as normal, but as always I'm always thrown when seeing the swim distance laid out before me.

I was used to swimming 200m loops, confident but well and truly in my comfort zone. Seeing the markers set out for the 1.5k of swimming in Cardiff Bay made for a similar reaction to when I first saw 750m mapped out. It's a fair old distance, but I just had to get on with it, stick to my pace and not panic. Previously this advice went out the window early on, but that day I held it together. By maintaining a steady rhythm I was able to hold my own, still eventually being overtaken by the stronger swimmers of the following wave, but at least I knew this was because of their prowess and not so much my inability to swim. Reaching the exit ramp once again ticked off a little win. I was a stronger swimmer, but always relieved I didn't have a mishap during that first leg. Olympic triathlon swim distance completed in 38 minutes.

Transitions are still and probably will forever be a painstakingly slow part of every race of mine. Some have this down to a fine art, to a matter of seconds. Watching the professionals is always impressive. The helmet is on as the wetsuit is whipped off, and that's it. They are out the transition zone hopping onto their bike straight into their shoes and off they go. I like to take my time, dry off, stick on some socks and get comfortable for the cycle. It took a total of 3 minutes 42 seconds from leaving the water to setting out on the bike. In retrospect that is 3 minutes too long. Taking my time? Taking the piss more like.

The bike section was up next, an extended loop of the sprint distance I was familiar with but more of the same flat, smooth tarmac that makes for fast cycling around Cardiff Bay. With a strong effort on the first loop I managed to make up a few places. Unable to draft due to national ITU rules, I was able to tuck down in the drops of my handlebars and stay aero for long periods of time on the straight sections. More time on the bike meant more need for fuelling the body, and it had to be more strategic. One bottle of electrolytes mixed with some sort of caffeinated powder was enough in liquid form.

Solid carbohydrates came in the form of a cereal oat bar at about half way through the cycle. With an energy gel to consume just before the run leg starts I calculate that it should be enough, knowing there was a drinks station at the halfway point of the run should I need refreshing. Balancing the right amount to maintain energy but to not bog you down is crucial and could make all the difference.

I got off the bike in 1 hour 20 minutes and I felt good. I was in a comfortable position, but all the places I had made up on the bike, were soon lost fart-arsing around in the transition area again. Change of shoes, sunglasses on and away I was on the start of a 10k run.

The run consisted of two laps of 5k, which meant it was pretty busy with the sprint distance triathletes (who started after the Olympic distance waves) on the same run route. This wasn't a problem, if anything it meant encouragement and support from more people. Having only stopped briefly for a quick swig of water at the halfway point I was back on my way towards finishing a decent 10k run leg.

The end of the run finished in typical fashion with some quiet reflection around the back of the Wales Millennium Centre to bank around to a cheering sprint finish. This time the sprint finish was down a blue carpet followed by a totally unnecessary leap over the finish line. Medal around the neck as I gasp for breath with my hands on my knees, it was done. My goal was reached. Chocolate biscuits in my mouth and a non-alcoholic beer in my hand, that was it! Total run time – 51 minutes.

The total time for my Olympic Distance Triathlon was 2 hours and 56 minutes. Just to put that into perspective, Alistair Brownlee won Triathlon Gold at the 2012 London Olympics with a time of 1 hour and 46 minute. So not too far behind him.

On to the 8th July 2018, the third and unfortunately final Velothon Wales event before the organisers realised it was no longer cost effective and decided to call it a day. That call was a huge disappointment for cycling fans as the 2018 version of this event had multiple distances for more cyclists to enter; it seemed to be popular too. With three different distances to choose from it was an easy decision to opt for the full 85 miles (136km). This year was the first time doing it on my own so I was in a position to pace it myself and limit any interference, I knew what to expect and other than a mechanical it was in the bag. What I hadn't bargained for was the relentless sun beaming down on us riders for the good part of 7 hours. Hydration was a big player in this game so I found it wise to squeeze an extra two litre bottle of water into the leg of my cycling shorts. It proved to be a life saver and I mean that quite literally.

About 40 miles into the sweat fest we were forced to stop for about 30 minutes down a narrow lane. We all immediately feared there had been an accident and prayed no one was seriously injured. As we stood around the heat increased and it all proved too much for one poor rider, who with a known condition fainted and entered into a stage of fit. She was alright in the end, her friends were well prepared, and plenty of space was given, as was my additional bottle of water. Where most people had some sort of electrolyte or caffeine mixed within their drinks bottles the smartest thing was to avoid consumption of that and take pure water. Surrendering my bottle was a no brainer. The crowd moved on and the true cause of the stoppage was revealed. Turns out that a local resident decided to set up an unofficial watering stop and was offering a top up of water bottles from the junction of his property. On the face of it, this was a heartwarming gesture; he was trying to look after the riders during this heat wave. However the consequential actions meant riders were left standing around, waiting for bottles to be filled from the man's hose. Daft when you think the first official rest area was less than 10 miles away.

The rest of the route was uneventful in terms of incident, which of course is a relief. The Tumble was only slightly easier with stronger legs, and Caerphilly mountain provided the same cheering crowds as to be expected. Finish time must have been around the 7 hour mark again, and I was alright with that.

On days like that, with the sun shining and a good few hours on the bike, it's glorious. Cycling at this level harbors community vibes and camaraderie. It is a shame this event no longer operates, but if the business model is unsustainable there's not much we can do. I'm grateful I was able to take part and see some sights of South Wales that I frequently return to.

Next up was 10 miles of borderline torture in the disguise as Tough Mudder in August of 2018. With what I thought was the end of my triathlon events for the year I pushed my time in the gym and prepared for more climbing, crawling, carrying and jumping. I was preparing for something that was on my bucket list for a while, but in all honesty, there's no real way to prepare for what lay ahead. You can watch all the videos you want, but ultimately you wing it on the day and hope you come out unscathed.

Tough Mudder isn't cheap, and seeing the scale of this event proves why. Arriving at the location feels like the start of a strange kind of festival where music is pumping and people of all shapes and sizes wearing all sorts of fancy dress. Some people are drinking, some dancing, everyone is having a good time. At least that was the atmosphere prior to the event starting.

This was another event attended on my own, I wasn't fazed by that as by now I'm used to getting on with what's in front of me, but by the time you've completed the warm-up you realise the same togetherness and camaraderie exists in the OCR (Obstacle Course Race) world as well as the triathlon world. The infamous Tough Mudder pledge solidifies that mentality during the warm up in the holding pen. A muscular bloke, who probably bench presses his own body weight for shits and giggles gets on the microphone and enthusiastically recites commandments straight out of the mud Bible, with his receivers repeating it back in equal manner.

"I UNDERSTAND THAT TOUGH MUDDER IS NOT A RACE BUT A CHALLENGE!!"

"I PUT TEAMWORK AND CAMARADERIE BEFORE MY COURSE TIME!!"

"I DO NOT WHINE - KIDS WHINE!!"

"I HELP MY FELLOW MUDDERS COMPLETE THE COURSE!!"

"I OVERCOME ALL FEARS!!"

I was pumped and felt unstoppable, I was ready to smash this event and have fun doing it. The gun goes off to a roar from the "mudders" and we head towards a big stack of hay bales, it was on!

Mid way through the route the sadistic course creators have their fun! "Arctic Enema" is a climb up 15ft of scaffolding to slide down a tube into ice cold water. Heart skipping beats and clothes soaked through with water, the next obstacle, if you can call it an obstacle, was given the title "Electroshock Therapy". This entailed a short dash through the mud, over bales of hay while trying to weave between the live strips of electrically charged wires. It's daft, it's questionable and not entirely necessary. Other than skip the obstacle on medical grounds there were a few options to get through this one. Option one was to crawl through the mud and risk being zapped in the face. Option 2 was to attempt a shimmy through the wires and risk getting zapped, fall to the ground and get zapped some more. Finally option 3 was to run as fast as you can and reduce the pain to the shortest amount of time. I opted for the latter.

With a deep breath I make like Colin Jackson, sprinting towards the danger, hurdling the hay bales and dodging what I could. It was looking heroic until I was stung by the last set of wires. The split second body paralysis sends me hurtling face first towards the mud, managing to channel some commando influenced evasion strategy I instinctively style out my fall by tucking in my head, land on my shoulders, embrace the mud and roll out through it. Standing straight back up in disbelief, to the cheers of the morbid onlookers, I check to see if there is any delayed injury and continue on to the next obstacle.

To end the challenge comes a 10ft inwardly arched wall to scale as best you can, with the help of ropes, other mudders or by skill. With my 6ft height and gangly limbs I wouldn't say skill played a part, but I was able to rocket up the ramp and grab the top ledge, making it look easier than it was.

By now I was totally knackered and fortunately the event was done and the challenge was dusted. Another well organised event full of equal amounts of fun and danger. I'm in no rush to do it again but I cherish those memories spent galloping round a field in Badminton, England. I still wear the finisher T-shirt frequently, just to remind me of how tough and muddy it really was.

I didn't get a T-shirt for finishing my next challenge; to be honest I could have done with a new pair of knees and shiny new arsehole!

Brixwhitch165 was up next, and this was straight out of the "stupid idea" box. I say Brixwhitch165 like it's a well known global event, have you not heard of it!? Of course you haven't, it's a poor attempt at a portmanteau, combining the words Brixton (suburb of South London) and Whitchurch (suburb of North Cardiff). The 165 represents the mileage between the two, and I was going to cycle it.

There is some added poignancy to this challenge and it's not as random as it seems. Remember this year was all about William, a friend who had passed away in 2017. Brixton was the last place he lived in London, before moving to Whitchurch in Cardiff to ultimately settle down. I thought it would be the right kind of challenge to honor his last migration, mixed with the right level of crazy to encourage people to dig deep and donate to this worthy cause in Williams' name.

The route would start out in Brixton and head towards Kew Gardens, pass Heathrow and on to Slough, then the A4 through Reading and pretty much all the way on that same road for the majority of the challenge until I reached Chippenham. The route would then head North West towards the Severn Bridge, to cross the border and then drop back down towards Newport after Chepstow, and then finish up in Cardiff. 165 miles, over two days. What could go wrong?

There was no way I would be able to do this completely alone so a support crew was required. I managed to rope in a friend from London to help me get to Maidenhead, 30 miles away from the start line. Another friend would join me for the Yate to Chepstow section (19 miles) and another mate would cycle would carry me home from Newport to Cardiff (20 miles). The challenge would be over two days with a stopover about halfway in the picturesque setting of Marlborough, this was where my girlfriend would greet me, after no doubt worrying every minute of the way.

What to pack for a long cycle? You would think I know by now having completed a number of cycles pushing 85 miles, you'd expect me to have the right gear, understand what works and what doesn't and have the learned knowledge on what happens to your body after prolonged cycling. Sure. All I really knew was that it was going to hurt.

With no official fueling stations along the route I had to think long and hard about what I needed, because of this it was likely that I would need to carry everything myself for each day. A concern was having to stop, chain up my bike to top up supplies. Therefore I opted to cycle with a backpack made for snowboarding and filled it up with as much as I could fit into it. With two drink bottles sitting in the bike cages I had another two litre bottle in the bag. This should see me through the first stint of 80*ish* miles. Food wise I had a gourmet selection of jam sandwiches, welsh cakes, malt loaf, sweets, chocolate and crisps. It wasn't healthy stuff, more a mixture of stodgy, sweet and salty snacks.

Also in the bag was a bike lock, a multitool, spare inner tubes, a puncture repair kit and a hand pump. I decided to pack a small first aid in case it all goes a bit Pete Tong, although in retrospect I'm not sure what a plaster would do should I come off the bike. All of this would and could be replenished at the halfway stage to top up the levels for day two.

Navigation was another curve ball I had to consider. The route was 70% uncharted territory, and even though half of that was on the A4, I still needed to remove the anxiety of going the wrong way. To do this I decided to buy and attach a phone pouch with a clear window front so I could display a route to follow turn by turn on my phone. This pouch also doubled up as extra storage for a battery pack and some additional supplies, and by supplies I mean sweets.

There's no way of adding excitement to this challenge. It was just cycling, and shit loads of it. Cycling out of South London early doors was a dream, there was no traffic, no pedestrians and you have the roads to yourself. It's bliss, until you near Heathrow where it's always busy! Cycling with my new friend Rhod made the first 30 miles easier and settled any initial nerves. The funny thing was that I had only met Rhod the night before, he was the flat mate of my friend I was staying with on the eve of the cycle. He heard what I was doing and more importantly *why* I was doing it, and decided to make last minute plans to visit his friend in Maidenhead. I'm forever grateful for that tow he gave me out of London, probably at a pace quicker than what I would have started with, but the safety in numbers really helped.

I say my goodbyes to Rhod at Maidenhead and set off alone with my thoughts for another 50 miles or so. I was in no rush, the weather was dry so I settled down at a steady pace and stayed comfortable. Having already consumed a few snacks and some liquid, I made the most of a beer garden just past Reading and had a proper sit down. The pub was closed as it was still relatively early, so no chance of a pint. I updated my progress with friends who were tracking my journey while filling up on sandwiches. I topped up my water bottles and added some electrolyte tablets to balance the lost salts and sugars, and after a quick pee behind the bush I was back on the A4 road.

The most exhausting thing about this cycle was not so much the distance, but everything else that comes with it. What I mean is cycling was the obvious part, it's easy to train for, you just jump on your bike and go cycling. What adds to spent energy consumption is the constant over thinking. Where am I? Am I going the right way? Should I stop and check? Am I visible enough? Is that car too close to me? Can that lorry behind me overtake? All while pedalling unfamiliar roads. Admittedly it all adds to the adventure but does make it all the more draining.

Fortunately the rest of the ride into Marlborough went without any incident. There were a few close calls with idiots driving too fast and a few tricky moments trying to urinate on the side of the road while wearing bib shorts. Other than that it was manageable. I descended into Marlborough a little ahead of schedule so capped off the day by stopping at a pub. It was early afternoon and the sun was shining, the lure of a refreshing pint was all too tempting. I parked the bike in the beer garden, asked a friendly looking couple to "keep eyes" and placed my order at the bar. Decked out in cycling gear the barman asked where I had cycled from, he's face skewed up when I answered Brixton. You can imagine his face when I said I was en route to Cardiff.

The temptation to have another beer in the sunshine didn't get the better of me this time; I still had about 8 miles to cycle to get to the B&B. Those 8 miles were the toughest of the day as my legs had started to seize up and I could now also feel the aches in my shoulders, neck and groin. I needed a bath, sharpish.

It was mid afternoon by the time I got to soak my aching body and start my recovery in readiness for the next day. I was helped into and out of the bath, carried out some stretches, managed a gentle hobble around the town, demolished a carb-heavy dinner and I was fit for nothing else. I had survived the first day without any issues but with rain expected for day two, I knew things wouldn't get any easier. My bag was packed, the alarm was set and I settled down for a restless night of cramp.

You know that feeling of closing your eyes for sleep and the alarm clock sounds seemingly moments after? That was this weekend, but no chance of playing the snooze game, I had to get up and get going. Shower, breakfast, some bike checks and I was waving goodbye to Marlborough. What lay ahead was 20 more miles of the A4 before I headed Northwest towards the Severn Bridge. I set off as quickly as possible to make the most of the dry weather, the rain was coming and it wasn't going to stop. Neither was I.

Strangely the downpour started the moment I turned off the A4, I said goodbye to the road that served me well and was greeted with non-stop rain. It is all well and good having a waterproof jacket but within half an hour I was soaked through. With the rain falling from above and occasionally from either side, the surface water found its way up into my socks, shoes, bib shorts and midriff. You get to the point where staying dry is beyond avoidable and you just embrace it. The elements were part of the challenge, fatigue was kicking in faster than I anticipated but with every push of the pedal I knew I was closer to the finish line. I was getting home, I might be ill afterwards but I was moving forward and at this point that's all that mattered.

Seemingly out of the blue, a ray of sunshine beams through the rain in the form of my good friend Harry. It was still raining but Harry provided the much needed morale boost and companionship. The cycle was getting lonely and it was good to have someone to talk to instead of myself and the occasional road kill. Harry lived in a small village North of Bristol called Tate but was originally from North Wales and had moved to Cardiff before heading over the bridge. He was perfectly situated for a much needed tow. Harry loved to be outside even in the rain, his positive attitude was inspiring and I soon forgot about any concerns I had.

Coincidently the Severn Bridge Half Marathon was taking part on the same day and happened to be kicking off about half hour before we made it to the bridge. A few friends were running this event, for the same cause as me, and it would have been great to see, cheer and wave them on. However the biggest concern at this point was that the road closures and diversions were potentially threatening to impede our river crossing. This would have been a bit of a kick in the balls as we didn't want to stand around in the rain and diverting up to Gloucester would have added at least 70 unnecessary miles to the route home.

Fortunately the last of the runners made it past our entry point and after sneaking through a few barriers we were able to cross the now fully closed, empty M48 motorway. Dreams of actually cycling on the motorway were dashed as even though it was closed we were instructed to use the pedestrian route, but even that was an eerie experience, being so quiet with only the wind and rain making a sound.

(The newer Severn Bridge, now called the Prince of Wales Bridge, isn't crossable by pedestrians – hence the reason for having to cross the original bridge Severn Bridge).

Over the bridge and into Chepstow Harry waves me off now having to cycle all the way back home in the continuous rain. I'm back on my own, once again grateful for the company during that stretch.

I push on and make it towards Caldicot and then hit Magor. Now Magor was a huge checkpoint for me as from here on in, I actually knew where I was going. The next 25 miles were made up of roads I had cycled many times before. This meant I had one less thing to worry about and focus energy on spinning the legs. Another guiding light came in the form of the person who got me into this cycling business, Thomas. He shows up, also completely soaked to the bone, but he's grinning like the Cheshire Cat, chuffed to see me and ready to lead me homeward bound.

The last leg was by far the most fun. Yes it was raining, yes I was tired, yes I was soaked through and in dire need of a lot of things, but I was almost at the finish line, which gratefully was a nice warm pub. I was cycling through my home town with one of my best mates egging me on every push of the pedal. The biggest challenge I had set myself was nearing the end. I had survived without any major accident, incident or mechanical failure. My noble steed was a joy to ride. It's not the lightest or fastest of bikes, but it managed every terrain, hill climb and pothole that came its way.

As we turned the last few corners Thomas dropped back and let me lead, he knew that some close friends and family were waiting outside the pub to cheer me in. I was expecting my girlfriend and maybe one or two friends, but seeing a small crowd really warmed up my soul. However knackered I was, however cold, hungry and depleted I was, getting off that bike and into the pub was like arriving at the pearly gates. There was a beer waiting for me and a few more behind the bar to help numb the pain. After cleaning up, changing into something other than Lycra and sitting on something more comfortable than a saddle, we toasted to William and thanked everyone who helped make this adventure possible. A special thank you goes to my girlfriend who not only drove the 160 miles, but worried non-stop for the whole duration. To be fair, we were both exhausted. During that weekend the total money raised increased considerably, and that was down to both the cycle and the Severn Bridge Half Marathon run by friends who were also at the pub, it was a lovely end to a great weekend of challenges.

On a personal note I had pushed my body further than it had ever been, it was getting fitter and stronger, and that is the same for my mentality. There were some low points during the 12 hours 20 minutes of cycling the 168 miles, the mind wandered to some strange places. Using the reason for the cycle in the forefront of my mind kept me going. A byproduct of that turned out to be foundation work for the biggest challenge of them all, I just didn't know it yet.

The year was not finished, by no means. In between getting electrocuted and cycling from London to Cardiff a friend entices me into signing up for a third triathlon of the year. This would take place at the end September, there wasn't much thinking about this, just take my money.

However, before that, a week after Brixwhitch165, 12 of William's Warriors still had a group 10k race to run in Cardiff. With a flat and fast route, plenty of supporters and some iconic landmarks thrown into the mix, it makes for a great event. You may think that after multiple half marathons, obstacle courses and a load of cycling that a 10k might be a step backwards, but I'm not too big for a 10k, it's an opportunity to start and finish an event with the gang. Plus, there are always means to push the challenge. For me, it was to complete the 10k in less than 50 minutes. I believed it was doable, I just hadn't officially clocked it, and today was going to be the day.

Pre-race preparations are as standard, eat a carbohydrate high meal the night before, get plenty of sleep and stay hydrated. The morning of the race was the tried and tested breakfast of porridge, fruit and again, stay hydrated. Pacing strategy, build up to a comfortable pace, hold it and then increase for the last kilometer. Always sprint finish, empty the tank and leave nothing out there. Even if you have nothing else to give, sprint. It may not *look* like a sprint, but you'll be moving faster than you were. Those last moments can be the difference between disappointment and a personal best. The race was executed precisely, perfect conditions and I experienced no issues. I crossed the line satisfied I had given it my best, chip time 51:56, I was devastated.

I got over it pretty quickly though, I had too. It was a pleasure to complete the event with close friends and have a sense of that camaraderie that I thrive on.

I was also reminded of the last few weeks of stress I had put my body through, with little time to recover. I was burning the candle at both ends, but I was blinded by the money raising crusade. I counted myself fortunate to be fit and able to participate in these events, and I didn't want to stop. With three weeks until the last event of the season, I needed a break, a break that would ignite a fire in my belly.

Transition

Last minute getaways are sometimes the best. When you book a holiday in advance you may have months and months of running through each and every possible moment you may or may not experience during your trip. A last minute break gets you straight into the action; you don't have the time to build expectations that could be dashed when you turn up to the destination. That's why they are the best. Without over thinking things too much, you get up and leave your life at home and head towards the unknown. I needed this, I also needed some time away from swimming, cycling or running. I still loved the disciplines, but I was exhausted. So what's the next best thing to physical exertion? How about watching 2000 others doing it instead?

Friday morning at home in Cardiff my girlfriend asks if I fancy visiting Tenby to watch Ironman Wales. It was a no brainer, Saturday morning we were heading west to Pembrokeshire, it wasn't too far, about 100 miles, I had cycled further than that the other weekend. That's how I gauge distance now, foot long sandwiches and cycle challenges.

Our B&B is in Lamphey, a lovely little spot about 9 miles away from the Tenby. It was the only place available; understandably everywhere else is booked up and sold out. Tenby itself was jam packed and as a spectator all you can do is take it all in, admire both the beautiful scenes of the coastal town and also the participants only a day away from swimming 1.4 miles, cycling 112 miles and running a marathon, all within 17 hours. The general mood was thick with excitement, nerves and fear, and I was experiencing them all myself. What is going on? I had not experienced an event on this scale before, thousands of people walked the town and Tenby was gearing up for an event on a global level. I didn't have a heart rate monitor on, but I knew my heart was beating faster because of it.

With no registration, course reconnaissance, race briefings to attend or last minute bicycle checks to do, we took the rare opportunity to enjoy ourselves. We chilled on the beaches, walked around the quaint shops, had some food and drank some beer. I thoroughly enjoyed the atmosphere in every place we found ourselves, even having dinner in a pub full of families and individuals taking part the next day was great fun. Surprisingly some of the racers were also having a beer which I thought was very ballsy. It was easy to identify the participants as they were either kitted out in Ironman branded t-shirts and hoodies, or wearing an Ironman wristband ready for the next day. What I found fascinating was seeing older individuals wearing t-shirts and caps from past Ironman Wales events and also from international races. Tallinn, Chattanooga, South Africa and I even saw a Hawaii Kona cap which for some reason got me going.

By 2018 Ironman Wales was globally recognised and drew in the crowds from around the world, but why? Tenby is a small seaside town in Pembrokeshire, alternatively known as Dinbych y Pysgod, the Welsh for "little town of fishes". It's a place steeped in ancient history with castle ruins, the town encased within stone walls and plenty of character to boot.

With three main beaches to choose from, the Ironman swim takes place on the North Beach, a sandy shoreline of 700m with the formidable Goscar Rock standing tall in the middle adding to the spectacle. The beach is a steep walk down from street level to the sand, the surrounding rocks makes the beach feel like some sort of arena. Fill it with thousands of people and it's an impressive amphitheatre.

Tenby was, at the time of writing this, in its eighth year of hosting the Ironman Wales event, and compared to others it is still relatively young. However, Ironman Wales is known for being one of the toughest courses on the calendar. The answer to why depends on who you ask, and where they come from.

Ironman Wales takes place in either September or October, a silly season for Welsh weather. Mixed with the unpredictable sea swimming conditions and torturous elevation gains for both the bike and run, you can soon find yourself battling with more than just an Ironman, conquering the Dragon in more ways than one.

Some say Lanzarote in the summer is tough due to the heat and amount of climbing mixed together. Some even say it's tougher to train for races that take part in the summer as it tends to mean a winter spent training with limited light and lower temperatures in the UK. Either way, 140.6 miles of moving in a forward direction takes a lot, and sitting there in a pub I was starting to feel like I was missing out on something, but that may have been down to the beers I had drank. It was time to get back to the B&B, everyone had an early start in the morning.

The swim started at 07:00, and to get there in time the alarm clock was set for not long after we eventually got to sleep. Due to road closures, parking in Tenby was non negotiable, we headed to Carew airfield where Ironman arranged a shuttle bus service into the heart of Tenby, we were cutting it close and once again my heart was pounding. With a short power walk up to the top of the beach we look down in time to sing one of the strangest renditions of the Welsh national anthem. I'm not sure if they do this at the start of all the events, but the Welsh are a proud bunch and with the sun rising we got involved without too much deliberation. The streets were crammed with spectators, as was the beach below. The beach was separated into starting pens, full of around two thousand individuals ready to race, and just as many cheering supporters on the sand, all ready for a long day ahead.

Countdown done, klaxon starts and hundreds of different colored swimming caps enter the water. From this vantage point you see the scale of the swim, two 1.2 mile loops with an Australian exit around Goscar rock in between. That means the swimmers have to clamber out of the water and run around the rock before starting another loop. This is already insane, and with last night's beer worn off I conceded that there was no way I would survive this swim. The cut off time was approaching, I was anxious just thinking about it. I was happy watching the white splashes of water move slowly out, around and back to dry land, impressed by the whole spectacle.

The pro athletes were out in seemingly no time at all, making their way up to street level and greeted by our cheers they headed off down the street to the transition zone. Moments later, after what would be a rather speedy change, they were on their bike and heading west into more of Pembrokeshire. For us it was a case of clapping, cheering and supporting all the swimmers out of their first leg. Some were looking strong, some already looked knackered, some smiling, some grimacing, some cheering along with us. Unfortunately some were still in the water with the cut off time limit of 2 hours 20 fast approaching. You're willing them on as much as you can, but know the time is ticking away. It's tough to watch, but convince yourself they knew what they were getting into and would no doubt be back to give it another bash the following year.

For us we moved to a vantage point to see some of the cyclists head off on their big 112 mile ride and start tracking their progress on the Ironman app. Being 09:30 in the morning there's not much to do other than have breakfast, relax and take it all in.

The hours tick by and Tenby is still buzzing with supporters waiting for their loved ones to come back, the streets are sectioned off making way for both the bike route and run route. With our bellies full of breakfast we met some friends and headed out of the centre to a vantage point where the big loop ends and the small loop begins. The big cycle loop consists of 70 miles of cycling, and the small loop is the remaining 42 miles. This is also a cutoff point and you have to be on your second loop by around 14:30.

Funny old thing watching a bike race, you wait for so long for the peloton to come past that when they fly by at record speeds it's almost not worth waiting for. Our vantage point proved a good choice as there was a constant stream of cyclists whizzing by. After coming down a hill the cyclists have to change gear and head up a hill. It meant plenty of time to pick out a person you have been waiting for, give them a big cheer and wave them back out of view.

I was also perfectly positioned to check out each and every type of bike that was cycling past us. It was like some sort of conveyor belt of stupidly expensive bikes, and naturally one caught my eye.

It's hungry work watching hundreds of fit triathletes cycling by our viewing platform, so back up to the town for some local fish and chips. It was 14:00 and unsurprisingly the pro-swimmers-turned-cyclists had now turned into runners, these were the professional athletes who do this as a day job, and it was clear. The technique, poise and pace these men and women carried was a thing of pure beauty. Some looked tired, but they all looked determined, and with the 2.4 mile swim and 112 mile cycle behind them, they were pushing their limits to get to that finish line. Just a marathon stood between them and that medal, preferable the medal for first place.

With so much going on it was difficult to keep track using the app, find the next best place to watch, weave through the crowds and keep an eye out for people we were now cheering for. We made a bold but understandable decision to stay out on the run route, sacrifice watching the winner cross the line to stick around and cheer on a friend who had just made it off the bike and had started his run. Up until now we didn't know he was actually racing, but it was good to see him and give him the boost he so desperately needed. Brian was looking strong but we could tell he was totally knackered, I could see the determination in his face that there was no way he would be beaten. With our loud cheers of support he waved us goodbye and off he trotted on the last leg of his day.

Missing the winner cross the finish line wasn't too disappointing, it may have been a blessing in disguise as what I witnessed next set the wheels in motion for the next chapter of my life and the start of my own Ironman journey.

Athletes were starting to finish the race, we knew this as the app was popping up with names that had run the red carpet. The South African Matt Trautman crossed the finish line first in a time of 8 hours and 53 minutes. That was quite an achievement in itself, but even more astonishing when you find out he is the first male ever to win Ironman Wales for a second time. Matt won it back in 2014. Broke his back in 2017 and came back to Wales in 2018 to secure his monumental comeback.

We decided to make our way to the finish line and cheer on some finishers. It was hardly a finish line, more like a red carpet finish line funnel, banked both sides with a cheering mob of supporters making one hell of a racket. The crowd were not necessarily supporting any one individual, just supporting anyone who managed to survive the day. The atmosphere was electric, and the finishers basked in their red carpet glory.

Luckily the female winner had not yet crossed the finish line, but we were just in time. After 10 hours and 7 minutes the multiple Ironman and triathlon winner Lucy Gossage crossed the line in powerful fashion, business first. Once through the finish line ribbon she didn't slump in a heap of exhaustion; she didn't bow her head for receipt of her medal, nor grab the nearest bottle of water. Instead she bounded, bounced, twirled and danced her way back up and down the red carpet with the biggest smile a human being could wear. We, the crowd, were lapping it up, loving every moment, sharing her joy. You could see the mixture of emotions in her face, jubilation, relief and acceptance. It wasn't her first win at Wales, but it may have been her last. It seemed she knew that there and then. That acknowledgment and acceptance of the inner peace she carried, it was a heartwarming sight. Lucy had posted on social media the day before that it may be the last time she wears the "Number 1" bib as her work and study as a cancer doctor had cut her amount of training time. What a human. What a hero.

Those moments were brilliant to watch, and moments I will personally treasure. Lucy was the icing on the cake for me. It was hook, line and sinker. I wanted those finish line feels, that joy and relief from a long day of swimming, cycling and running. From the moment I arrived in Tenby I was swaying with my own belief of whether or not Ironman was achievable for me. It honestly had not even registered on my radar a week before. Seeing all sorts of shapes, sizes, ages and abilities around the course that day started the embers inside of me. Seeing how challenging the course was sparked the flame and cheering Lucy down the finish line funnel was like adding fuel to the fire that was by now already ablaze. Ironman was the missing piece of the puzzle that would cap off my own triathlon journey. We decided to leave shortly after celebrating the female finishers as being a Sunday we had to get back home for work the next day. Coincidentally, so did Lucy.

The trip home was a blur, it had been a long weekend, and full of inspiration. All I wanted to be from that moment on was an Ironman, and I was willing to pay the price.

Before anything else, there was a small matter of the last minute sprint distance triathlon that my good buddy Ron encouraged me to sign up for. It was now the end of September, it was dark, and it was cold. It was wet and it was windy. There was no carnival atmosphere of Tenby, far from it. This was a grassroots triathlon event in an old quarry full of swans. The surrounding roads were terrible and the run route might as well have been cross country. To be honest, I could have done without it, but it proved an important part of the journey that I'm unable to forget, but for all the wrong reasons.

Early race starts in September mean racking up your bike and arranging your transition area before sunrise. Not only was I having to deal with the standard level pre race nerves, they were somewhat heightened by the fact I couldn't see much but for the torch light on my phone. The bike racks were not numbered so that was a bonus, but the last minute checks on the bike and questionable visual assurances were far from ideal. Anxiety levels high, I was already spending unnecessary energy with an hour to go before race time.

What made matters considerably worse was the fact that the only available toilets on site were in fact locked. Picture 300 nervous triathletes, having woken up early to have breakfast and maybe even a coffee, an hour before the race begins, unable to use a toilet. It was shit.

When nature calls, you have to answer. A last minute addition to my race bag happened to be my own supply of toilet roll and bags. It wasn't pretty but it had to be done, and a lot of other people answered the same call that morning. I had to focus, the race brief consisted of common rules and regulations about drafting, open roads and course routes. We were then split up into waves and we were ready to roll.

The swim start required us to get into the water before the gun sounded for each wave. This was the warmest part of the whole race and if it wasn't for the amount of swan shit floating around I could have stayed in there all morning.

The gun sounds and away we go. 18 minutes of a few left and right handed turns of swimming in a quarry and it's over, we exit the water by climbing out using a cargo net and make the painful journey barefoot across the gravel to the transition area, everything is there waiting for me, soaking wet.

I strip out of a wet wetsuit; I put on some wet cycling gear and hit the open road, literally. Triathletes taking part in races don't always have exclusive rights to the road, and I totally understand that. In previous experiences a closed road event does cost a little more. The open road had to be accepted and it was a case of ploughing on, dealing with other drivers, traffic, pedestrians and even a roadside hedge cutter which caused disruption on both loops of a cycle route. With the route twice out and back there was not much of an atmosphere, although saying that my head was tucked down as much as possible to avoid the rain and to stay as aero as possible. I was about as aero as a brick in all honesty.

Unsurprisingly there were not that many supporters lining the wet roads, but heading back towards the start/finish line and seeing a small crowd of supporters, even though not necessarily for me, did provide some warmth to my numb body.

Transition two, nothing was dry. I changed my wet cycling shoes for wet running trainers and decided to keep my cycling jersey on. It contained the details of the Velindre hospital on the back as further publicity and exposure to the charity I was racing for. It was also soaking wet and I would have struggled to remove it.

The overwhelming feeling, or lack thereof at the start of the 5k run was that for the love of me, I could not feel my feet. They were so cold that it was a battle of brain power to convince myself that my feet were actually attached to my legs and trust the fact they would hit the ground at each stride. It was all too easy to react based on feeling, and think that my legs were shorter than they were. This would have resulted in falling over multiple times. It was one of the strangest feelings experienced during an event, but I managed stay upright and soon find some feeling in my toes.

Pushing on over a range of terrains, through trees, dodging dog walkers and finding it difficult to pace this run, it was another case of just finishing. I was in no position to challenge, it was purely a case of getting this done, and I just wasn't in the mood.

At the finish line I was greeted by cheers from my loved ones, they were happy they no longer had to stand about in the rain anymore. Crossing the line I was given a banana, one of those shiny foil blankets that help keep the warmth in and the last medal of the year. We didn't hang around long, a cup of tea and a few biscuits inhaled, it was time to get home and thaw. I wasn't too bothered about analyzing my race to the level of splits, but a notable take away from that race was that Ron had done very well, and it was great seeing the triathlon bug take another bite from him.

This triathlon goes down as the least enjoyable triathlon of them all, enough to turn some people off for life. Strangely enough all I could think about was Ironman Wales; the hobby was turning into an obsession even though I had just lost my soul to a local sprint distance triathlon. I had just finished the worst event in terms of enjoyment, but sometimes a triathlon event and triathlon as a sport just isn't pretty. It can rain, people might not turn up to support and there might be swan shit in the water, but it is all part of the fun and games in the long run. It capped off the third triathlon of the year and a number of other events that overall went considerably well, and in that respect, contrary to how that last triathlon unfolded, I realised that I actually loved it.

I wasn't quite done with triathlon for 2018, there was still a challenging swim, a grueling cycle through some lava fields, and a run that starts in the blistering heat and can finish well into the night. I wasn't taking part in this, I either wasn't good enough or couldn't afford it, probably both. It was the 42nd edition of the Ironman World Championship in Kailua-Kona, Hawaii, and it was being streamed online.

Due to the time differences it meant the event started at around 17:00 (BST) Saturday evening, which was perfect. I could watch pro's set off on the swim, watch some of the cycle, go to bed not too late and wake up at sunrise to watch the last of the runners cross the finish line. Snacks lined up, I was ready to go.

I switched it on and I was instantly hooked. This was like Tenby on an even bigger scale, some sort of triathlon show with an American glow and enthusiasm you would expect to see in Hollywood, all mixed with a seemingly spiritual connection to triathlon.

Ironman was born in Honolulu, Hawaii back in the 70's, the brainchild of husband and wife, John and Judy Collins from California. Combining local events they tie swimming, cycling and running together, "Whoever finishes first, we'll call them the Ironman" – declared Mr Collins.

Now steeped in traditions and ceremony, Kailua-Kona Ironman hosts the annual World Championship which pulls in all the qualifiers from Ironman events held globally. Not only are there professionals here, but the age groupers that grabbed top spots in a previous event and also the individuals who had raced 12 Ironman events gaining a legacy spot at Kona. There are other ways to get to Kona, but they involve spending a lot of money. However you get there, Ironman Kona is the Mecca for triathletes and I admire anyone who takes part.

The coverage included interviews with racers, previous winners, local legends and triathlon aficionados. The broadcasting of this race was organised as well as the whole event, showcasing the broad spectrum of what Ironman and triathlon is all about. Which leads on to diversity in triathlon, or maybe the lack thereof? Which leads on nicely.

As diverse and inclusive triathlon claims to be, based on personal experience it feels that there is a misrepresentation of the world we actually live in. Be it taking part, supporting or volunteering, from a personal view and being mixed race myself, I've noticed that a lot of, if not all of the swimmers, riders and runners are white.

This of course is not a problem, but it does beg the question, with the UK being a multicultural nation, and with triathlon being this all inclusive, diverse "fastest growing" sport - where are all the people of colour? I don't have the answers, and even if I did, I doubt it's not straightforward to pinpoint.

There's no preaching here, just an honest observation and an attempt to open discussions and trigger a thought process over the swim, bike and run sport.

The whole "black people *can't* swim" notion is a stereotype that is steeped in racism and dates back to segregation, a time where black people were not allowed to swim in local venues, or with white people. Not being allowed to swim in local bathing areas sets a recurring and ingrained misconception that black people *couldn't* swim. Nowadays, and in the UK at least, it is believed that a large percentage of black people cannot swim and unsurprisingly make up a large number of deaths relating to drowning. Has the lack of actively encouraged swimming over generations led to this dangerous statistic in the 21st century?

Clearly learning to swim isn't just recreational; it's survival. The *real* type of survival.

Questions around cultural mindset, the cost of learning to swim and the lack of black swimming role models contribute to the lack of uptake.

The same can be said about cycling and with its opposite views towards pedal power. On one hand, cycling can be seen by some as a lower class mode of transport. If you cycle a push bike it means you can't afford to drive a car. Ludicrous right!? But a carbon framed, top end group set, dropped handlebar road bike out prices many people, regardless of colour, out of wanting to cycle. Of course we know there are bikes ranging in price, but without appropriate guidance from representatives from different communities, the thought of recreational cycling or even racing, may not even register.

When RideLondon admitted to digitally adding a picture of a black woman into an image of cyclists to appear "diverse" it kick started a whole new level of conversation. Even though there may be a serious lack of representation I also think attitudes are changing.

The impression that cycling road bikes and wearing Lycra is an activity for middle-aged white men is becoming old news. There are initiatives and schemes to push cycling out to the masses. In the UK the growth of the Black Cyclist Network has opened their doors to everyone, but fronted by a black Londoner of Ghanaian heritage the mission is to connect cyclists from black and minority ethnic backgrounds. State side there is a growing number of both cycling and triathlon groups with their main aim to encourage inclusion. Representation is there, but you have to look for it and until true organic representation becomes mainstream, Joe Public will continue to see the same thing.

Then on to running, another entity and rabbit hole altogether. Over the years long distance running, middle distance track distances and sprinting have made black superstars from all over the world, both male and female. With Olympics, World Athletic events and Marathons beamed directly to terrestrial TV sets, exposure and role models are easy to come by. From Jessie Owens and Tommie Smith to Michael Johnson, Usain Bolt and Sir Mo Farah. Denise Lewis, Cathy Freeman and Shelly-Ann Fraser-Pryce, and personal favourites of mine, Linford Christie and Colin Jackson. The list goes on.

TV is still a major player where youngsters find idols, but swimming, cycling and running fall far down the list compared to football, rugby, basketball and even boxing.

Just to add, triathlon *is* available for everyone, but it's not *for* everyone, and just because I love it, it doesn't mean that everyone else should too. As suspected, I just have the questions and maybe over the years the answers will come. I don't believe there are groups set up to purposely exclude someone based on their race, beliefs or even sex, but maybe more needs to be done to openly encourage individuals from all backgrounds to get involved. As long as triathlon keeps pushing diversity and inclusion more people will be encouraged to give it a go, organically or otherwise. There will be swimming, cycling and running groups that openly encourage riders from different backgrounds and naturally role models will be born. Rome wasn't built in a day, and neither will a frequently diverse start line.

Game Changer

After a week off from any sort of physical exertion, it was time to level up. The last few years I had been slowly building confidence in my ability and strengthening my mindset. I was achieving goals that I never thought were possible, the belief was growing and I put that down to consistency and the people around me. With a strong circle of friends, encouragement from individuals and support from my swimming teacher James, I was in the perfect position to enter into unknown territory and commit to entering an Ironman. This was ramping up the "let's see what happens" mantra big time.

But before I can I make any decision, I needed to consult my 1 woman support team. Even though I'd be putting myself through the rigorous training just to get to the start line, it was my girlfriend who would also have to endure the unrelated consequences. I wasn't asking for her permission, but more of a blessing to commit myself to this challenge, and to pull her along with me. After an open and honest discussion it was decided, but in all fairness she already knew I was itching to do it. While at Tenby, watching the entertainment unfold, she had front row seats in seeing my belief growing. She knew what was coming, and with nothing but love, she joined me on that journey.

James was a multiple Ironman finisher but got his kicks by helping others achieve their goals. James had been pumping Ironman since the day I met him but thought he was just blowing smoke up my arse. He saw the potential and ignored my lack of self belief, and even with the Olympic distance triathlon being my goal, James was working on something different, James was laying the groundwork in preparation, unbeknownst to me.

Not long after watching the incredible Hiromu Inada of Japan, at the age of 87 cross the Ironman World Championship finish line in Kona after 16 hours and 53 minutes, it was time for me to get my arse into gear. James and I met for a coffee and the conversation was short, I stated I wanted to become an Ironman, his response was short and simple, "let's get to work then!". Easy.

People approach Ironman in two ways; either get a coach, follow their coach's plan, have that support and use them to lean on in times of issues. The other half buy the books, research online or wing it. I needed accountability because left to my own devices I would have either caused injury (although not avoidable), burnt out by over training, or not pushed hard enough and lost sight of the goal. I needed someone to keep me focused, Ironman is a big commitment and I didn't want to balls it up. So with that truth nugget, James became my official coach.

What I was doing with my body was one thing, but what I was putting into it was another. I had to seriously consider a change made back in June to my nutrition. There are a whole range of articles, documentaries, films, sports men and women pumping all sorts about what to eat and what not to eat. High this, low that, what was all the fuss about? I was curious, and based on curiosity alone; I decided to cut out meat from my diet for no other reason than I wanted to see what would happen. Would I still be able to swim, bike and run as fast, or even faster on a meat free diet? Does a meat free diet elongate recovery times from training sessions? Fast forward a few months of removing meat from my plate and to be honest I couldn't really tell the difference. I was still able to swim, cycle and run with no noticeable difference that the lack of meat was needed. I didn't miss the taste of meat either, so I decided to continue with a pescatarian diet.

Kicking meat out of my diet didn't mean I was now a plant eating health machine, I was still consuming a range of high carb meals and sugar loaded snacks. It was mixed with healthy additions full of protein, nutrients and food sources that I knew were good for me. It was a balance, and it was working. It also helped that my girlfriend was a great cook, which meant I didn't have to think too much, just eat.

With an upgraded mindset and belief, I needed to upgrade my gear. First up was my sports watch. A handy piece of kit, and for the last 6 months I had been using a Fitbit Ionic performance watch. It logged steps, runs, cycles and more attractively pool swims. However, the issue I had was it didn't log open water swimming, something I would be doing a lot more of in the next 12 months. Therefore I returned the watch and upgraded to a Garmin 735XT multisport watch, this changed the game. Not only was it logging the expected steps, runs and cycles, but also calories, heart rate and open water swimming. The watch also had the added benefit of automatically synchronising activities with the fitness tracker called Training Peaks.

Training Peaks was the application used by my new coach James, he was able to set a bespoke training plan for the full week, covering swim/bike/run activities as well as strength work, recovery sessions and rest days. Once an activity was recorded and uploaded to Training Peaks, James was able to break down performance metrics, provide feedback and adjust my plan accordingly. I could see my work load each week; I would post an activity and communicate how it went. It acted as an additional layer of accountability to keep me on track.

Next on the list was looking at the trusted noble steed, it was time to upgrade my bike. The Specialized Allez bike had served me well, better than I could have imagined and I had experienced some great adventures on the bike. It was there when I started my triathlon journey, completed three Velothon events and also got me from London to Cardiff, plus all of the training in between. For Ironman I believed I needed a competitive edge, cycling 112 miles of a notoriously difficult cycle route on an aluminum framed bike is totally achievable, but I needed to be as powerful as I could so I was in the market for a lighter, carbon frame bicycle.

I was faced with two options; sell my Specialized Allez Sport that had served me well for the last few years and use that money for a new bike. Or exercise the n+1 rule and consider how many bikes I actually need. I would say most cyclists (and the partners of cyclists) know the n+1 rule, where *n* equates to the number of bikes you own and therefore *+1* results in how many bikes you *should* own.

Of course this is total bullshit, own as many or little bikes you like, but it was the equation that got the better of me. This meant I was able to use the Specialized aluminum bike for winter riding and indoor training sessions, and use the new carbon kid on the block for some serious road training in more forgiving elements.

My window shopping at Ironman Wales left me with a shortlist of possibilities which included a mixture of aero bikes, TT bikes and triathlon bikes. The deciding factors in my decision were simply price and versatility. The 112 miles of the Ironman Wales bike route included nearly 8202ft of elevation (2500m) and taking place in Wales there's always a possibility the roads could be wet. I therefore couldn't justify buying a full time trial (TT) or triathlon bike. I also wasn't an age grouper pushing for a championship place in Hawaii. A road bike would do, and would also allow me to not look like a dick during weekend social group rides to a coffee shop.

The new bike in question was a 2018 Giant Propel Advanced 1. With an advanced-grade carbon composite frame and forks, Shimano Ultegra 11-speed group set, Giant P-A2 Aero wheelset and tubeless tires it came in at a pretty penny. Research was conducted solely online, and impatiently, after zero reconnaissance missions to any bike stores for a physical check, I clicked a few buttons on a website and my order was placed. Bike arrived the same week, with no real time to question the price; it was all soon forgotten during its first spin. New pedals on and straight out of the door, it was noticeably lighter than my now older bike and dangerously responsive. It was faster than expected and it would take a while to get used to how it handles. With a new bike comes new pedals, shoes and a helmet to match the carbon smoke green finish.

I also needed to upgrade my running trainings, but not for a better brand, or for ones that made me think I was running faster, I merely updated to the latest version of my existing pair. A year ago I had visited a shop that specialises in all things running, and to assist with finding the best fitting shoe, you have access to a treadmill to demonstrate your running gait. High arch, overpronation, underpronation, wide toe box, slim foot, flat foot. All the metrics of your feet are checked and a series of expensive trainers are pushed your way. Running half marathons and the training that goes with it means it is well worth investing in your runners. Therefore, over the years that followed my first visit, I would continue to buy the same pair of trainers, but whatever version was available at the time. It was an easy continuation to make. I still wear a Mizuno Wave Inspire running shoe to this day.

I was recklessly burning through cash like there was no tomorrow, both a new bike and coach were monthly expenses that were manageable, but combined with the cost of the Ironman entry fee and I was seriously pushing my budget to its limits. If only I could stop giving my bank balance a hammering, but it didn't stop there.

A triathlon season as an amateur isn't cheap, you have your "A race" that you shape other events around as support and they can soon add up. Ironman costs a few hundred pounds, and once you enter, there's instant pressure to make the most of your money. There was a deferral option, but that wasn't a consideration at this point. 2019 *had* to be the year.

In order to get my training off to a purposeful start I needed to set in stone the events leading up to my A Race - Ironman Wales. With 2.4 miles of swimming, 112 miles of cycling and another 26.2 miles of running it was no easy feat, and I wanted to give myself a fighting chance on race day.

My 2019 event timetable was planned as follows:

26th May – SWYD Sprint Triathlon in Barry

23rd June – Cardiff Olympic Triathlon
7th July – Long Course Weekend Wales (Swim Wales)
14th July – Swim/Run event in Barry
15th September – Ironman Wales

It was at this point that I made the conscious decision not to associate these events with a particular charity. Even though I could harness the donations and encouragement, Ironman was a huge event for me and I was already under a lot of pressure just to finish. With a lot more at stake I didn't think it was fair on a charity, myself or anyone who would sponsor me. I could only direct the thoughts of kind donations to individuals completing other events for other charities. Ironman was for me.

Goals set and I was ready to roll, but something had to give, and for me that was football. I had only recently started playing recreational 5-a-side football with a few friends I've known since college. They were pretty good and knew what they were doing; naively I thought that as I've done some running and incorrectly assumed I was generally fit, that a social activity would be great fun. Meeting every Sunday mornings for an hour kick about, what could go wrong!? Well a lot could have gone wrong. I managed a few weekends of attempting to play football but in all honesty it was a disaster. My body just wasn't used to the stop-start, slight contact demands of football. Having to move in different directions in quick succession just didn't fit my fitness. It was great fun and I loved the social aspect of it all, but the following day I was always hobbling around with aches and pains, which kind of hampered my training for the start of that week. It took its toil and the realisation of being only a dodgy tackle away from a bad knock on the knee or a twist of an ankle was the deciding factor to hang up my Astroturf boots. I could not afford to jeopardise my goals playing football and had to take things seriously.

Focus man, Focus!

I had 11 months to get to the start line of Ironman Wales 2019 on North Beach, Tenby. With a trainer on board and a structured plan, I was heading in the right direction. Even with a few years experience of swimming, cycling and running James and I decided to start from the beginning and build on what I had. It made sense, with races set in the calendar we were able to build accordingly in readiness for September. It also meant the stress load wasn't too grueling over Christmas and New Year.

January and February ticked along nicely, averaging 10 hours a week I was mixing strength work, yoga and stretches along with the usual swim, bike, run activities. Even those were being mixed up to add variety. Let's be honest, running on a treadmill can be boring. You're running in the same spot, looking at the same thing but mix in some structure allowing for efforts at different speeds and things can get a bit spicy.

Cycling efforts on the bike were a mixture of using the bikes in the gym, some sessions on the turbo trainer and out on the open roads when the weather allowed, which wasn't that often. The variety of options added a mixture of training sessions. The gym bike wasn't anything special, but it did give the opportunity to set resistance, clock distance and duration. Right next to a treadmill it allowed for quick transitions to running and I was able to repeat as a multiple brick session. The turbo trainer was used for more of an endurance session with the outdoor bike for bagging some actual distance to break up the cabin fever. I was still attending the swim sessions in the 50m pool each week, and occasionally popping into the leisure pool to see my elderly friends and update them on my progress. Still my biggest fans.

It was all going well, but a series of ill calculated decisions totally derailed my progress, and started an early downward spiral. I got injured.

I'm unable to categorically pinpoint the reason for picking up this injury, but I have a pretty good idea. Training was going well and the load on the body was about right. Some days I was more tired than before but I kept moving forward, communicated this with James and everything was under control.

Late February I took the opportunity to get an expert bike fit from an ex-professional cyclist, a previous Paris-Roubaix winner and this guy knew his stuff. After some introductions and fanboying from me, I get hooked up to a 3D motion capture tracking device, with a bunch of sticky balls over my body that display a digitally rendered version of my body on his computer screen. He is able to calculate my ideal cycling position making me "as one" with my bike and after a number of adjustments he was done. With some additional cycling advice, hints and tips I left inspired and excited that my efforts would be maxed out on my newly fitted bike.

One of the adjustments included the height of my seat post. Even though I found it comfortable to ride, I was told that to maximize output the new height would be more efficient. Of course I believed him, I had no reason not to and this wasn't the reason for my injury. What I did when I got home may have been the reason.

At this point I had set up the *old* bike on an indoor turbo trainer, nothing special, just a typical magnetic roller with adjustable restriction settings. It was enough to get the legs spinning and handy for practicing transitions and brick sessions.

Trying to mimic the newer aero cycling position adopted on my fitted bike, I make similar adjustments to the seat height and handlebars. I test it out with a few rotations of the pedals and think nothing of it. Seemed alright.

Cycling on a bike, wearing shoes clipped into pedals, on a seat that is now too high for a considerable amount of time will result in a discreet strain on parts of your body, and in my case, my left Achilles tendon.

The pain didn't arrive suddenly, I felt a slight niggle coming on but it had taken far too long to realise how serious it could be. I ignored my body and cracked on with cycling, big runs and frequent dips in the pool, hoping it would just sort itself out. It was only after a few days that a little swelling occurred on my Achilles and made a strange creaking sound when I moved it. It was one of the sounds that goes through a person, like nails scratching on a chalkboard. It still makes me wince now thinking of it.

Frustrated, I thought winging it would be the best remedy. I apply ice and then heat and keep it moving. I was looking online and with no clear therapy I hobbled and hopped for four weeks, drinking anti-inflammatory root vegetable tea, massaging my foot with a cricket ball and cursing my whole situation. I was frustrated and a bit glum, everyone in my triathlon social circle were starting to push the training loads, with nice weather I saw their rides were more frequent and cycling to distant locations and I couldn't manage the stairs without discomfort. Pity party for one.

Sometimes the answer is staring right in front of you and this intervention came from home. My girlfriend ignored my pleas to save money and self medicate, and booked me in to see a sports physiotherapist. Reluctantly I agreed, but with nothing else working it was the call I should have taken a few weeks prior.

For me this whole experience was very strange. I walked into a room set up with multiple beds sectioned by hospital ward-like curtains, each containing people with all sorts of sports related injuries. I tell the physio my issue and within two minutes I once again find myself hooked up to a machine, but this time I was laying face down on a bed with some sort of microwave machine zapping my ankle. To my relief and according to the physio, this was common tendonitis, and more importantly, it was treatable. I needed three sessions of his microwave therapy and had to follow his strict instructions. I was told not to run or cycle but swimming was good. To give my ankle the support it needed, I was told to wear my running shoes everywhere. That was fine for the supermarket and general errands, but it made for strange looks at social events and standing at the office printer.

It took about eight weeks from aggravating my Achilles tendon to running without any pain, and it was eight weeks to remember. I had been blind to setbacks as I had managed to just plod on through this whole experience and avoid an injury. The training was never too stressful to potentially cause a two month hiatus. Remembering that your body can break is a lesson worth learning, and taking a step backwards can be painful, but also breeds time to reflect. It was only eight weeks, but without really knowing when you will return to full recovery you think the road is long. Staying positive was key, I was still passionate about triathlon and it gave me time to take in other aspects of the sport.

During this time my girlfriend and I attended the London Triathlon Show in the Excel centre. My obsession levels increased, with all the brands, stalls, demonstrations and talks, I was in my element. I loved listening to Louise Minchin, the BBC Breakfast show presenter who found triathlon a little later than some, and turned out to be an absolute beast of a triathlete. I was fully invested into hearing how she represented Great Britain and her plans of taking part in the notoriously brutal Isklar Norsman event.

Just a note on Norsman, this is the triathlon that starts at 05:00 by jumping off the back of a ferry into the cold waters of a Norweigen Fjord. In-freaking-sane!

I got some nutritional advice from Joe Beer, some advice on cycling shoes from the guys at Fizik and picked up some bargains and freebies along the way. I got to share the event with inspiring athletes and got to chat with organisations doing great things, for both triathlon and the environment.

A highlight was also seeing the bike Patrick Lange rode to win the 2018 Ironman Championships in Kona, Hawaii. I say bike, it might as well have been an anti-aircraft missile. It was a weapon; the aggressive aero design was beyond belief. The bike was secured to the stand it was on, but no doubt it was as light as a feather.

The whole day was excellent, a much needed pick-me-up during the down days of a dodgy ankle. It made me realise the reach and scope of the sport and all the moving parts that make it a global society, a really expensive movement.

A few weeks later and I was back, with my seat lowered.

The training plan picked up where it left off, and with my first event fast approaching I didn't really have time to start from the beginning again. However my fitness was outed pretty quickly, my swimming was decent and my cycling wasn't too far off the pace, but the running was a slog. There was also a thought of caution in the back of my mind; I felt I couldn't afford to have another setback so the best approach to my now weakest discipline was to rebuild the running in a sensible way. Cue the pun, step by step.

I wasn't quite back to running around the block, but my running was kept to a gentle pace and consciously making an effort to ignore duration and distance. I was frustrated, but I knew I would get back to my previous performance. Plus, with no sight of the returning Achilles issue, my confidence was growing by the day. This was both a boost mentally for me, and also a relief for my girlfriend who no longer had to put up with my irritable mood.

If I was still frustrated with my running, I must admit it was the complete opposite with my swimming. My relationship with swimming was strong. I was at a stage where other than completing drill sets of speed efforts, using flippers or a kick float, I was able to switch off and just swim. The goal in the pool was always to make sure I could swim the 2.4 miles within the permitted time. With these long sessions it was distance over speed, I trusted speed would come as a byproduct of consistency. With that approach I was able to get into the pool, turn off the world around me and have one objective. Swimming lap after lap of a 50m pool at a comfortable pace meant my breathing was steady and my body was moving without any disruption. Lap after lap would pass by and if it wasn't for my Garmin keeping score, I would have lost count. To me, this was a form of meditation, or mindfulness. My body would leave the pool tired, but my mind was at ease.

The more time spent swimming lap after lap in the pool, the more my understanding of swim etiquette grew. The old school standard rules still applied, no bombing, don't wee in the pool and no heavy petty. With lane swimming there are some unwritten rules that you're either told, or in my case learned the hard way.

Sometimes the lanes will state slow, medium or fast and will sometimes show the direction to be followed, being clockwise or anti clockwise. It gets tricky when they don't have the instructions. First in the lane, you call the shots. I've found many a morning where I've been able to pick an empty lane and dictate the rules. I'm able to comfortably get the swim toys out and spend a few laps conducting drill sets and happily take up the whole lane. If someone wants to join, I'll most probably switch to swimming anti-clockwise as breathing out of my right side I'm able to follow the guide ropes easier. The newcomers must adopt my direction and understand that the pace is somewhat unknown. Naturally they should leave a gap and if they are super speedy, they should overtake at a suitable time when it's safe to do so. If the lane gets busier, your session could go either way. Either you're somehow caught up in a fast lane where you are being overtaken frequently, or the opposite. Unless you're lucky enough to have a lane by yourself, your swim session can always be disrupted but someone else, understanding that is crucial. A big no-no would be jumping into a fast lane and proceeding to carry out some kick drills or pedestrian breast stroke and cause chaos. Sounds criminal, but I've seen it done.

With the days getting longer, warmer and more importantly dryer, my exercise on the indoor turbo trainer were coming to an end, and I was glad! Cycling in the spare room of an apartment, with just enough floor space for the bike, a propped up laptop and a desktop fan, wasn't ideal, but it surely did the job. Able to prepare clothes, water bottles and snacks the night before, I was able to crawl out of bed the next morning and straight onto the bike before I was fully awake.

Sessions on the turbo trainer can be excruciating without any visual stimulation. A quick hour in the saddle can seem like five, and a five hour session was a Saturday morning I won't forget in a hurry. Whether it was easier to blast out an hour or because a storm scuppered plans, I found the static cycling more bearable by watching videos on YouTube, Netflix or by popping on a DVD. There were plenty of options online to distract me from how mind numbingly boring it can be sweating out in a box room. Sweat was another issue. Without the natural flow of air circling my body as it normally would do on an outdoor cycle, clothing soon became damp with sweat as the heat ramped up, so it was vital to maintain hydration levels. It was also important to ensure I didn't sweat all over the bike as salty water can be problematic to bike components.

My repaired body soon caught up to the physical demands of the training plan as the week's workloads increased. I was back to myself, taking each day as it comes and ensuring I stretched after every session – something that is easily forgotten or ignored.

A twist of fate gifted a chance to visit a place I'd soon call my second home and check out the Ironman Wales course. Due to a holiday in Canada being cancelled the next best thing was Tenby, it made sense, and to be honest it should have been the top of our list in the first place. Both my girlfriend and I loved Tenby, and after the Ironman show back in September we were looking forward to returning and staying more central.

After asking nicely and promising a fancy meal, I was allowed to bring my bike along with us. I felt like a kid asking and that was because I was super excited. I actually got the opportunity to cycle some of the 112 miles of the Ironman Wales course, there was no way I was going to attempt the whole course, but I'd take a few miles of it no problem. This was only on another proviso that I wouldn't be back too late so we could both enjoy some downtime and explore. Perfect.

It was a Saturday morning and after arriving in Tenby the previous evening I was up early with excitement. At 06:30 I was already on the road, my recently purchased Garmin Edge cycling computer was mounted to my bike with the route preprogrammed ready for me to follow. The route was straight forward enough; 10 miles out of Tenby to Pembroke, head south towards Bosherston and follow the road west to Angle. You can't really go wrong from there as you loop around Angle and you find yourself back on the road you left not so long ago. Follow that back towards Pembroke, through the town and back on the same road again to Tenby. With still a lot more cycling on top of that, this route was a nice slice of what is known as the big loop, fortunately for me my first reconnaissance mission avoided some of the brutal climbs.

The early morning 45 mile cycle took around 3 hours, and I thoroughly enjoyed it. Not knowing what to expect I kept the cadence at a leisurely pace and took in the surroundings. This section of the course does vary quite a bit and at times I questioned whether I was on the right route. The road conditions go from your typical British single carriageway, where vehicles can whizz past at 60mph, with the only bonus being that they are nice and smooth. The other end of the road spectrum is a toss-up between tight lanes of chopped up tarmac or a concrete road as you cycle past operational army barracks, tanks and a firing range. Freshwater West, was a mixture of the whole lot and with a sprinkling of some sand. This part of the route meets the coast, with a side wind whipping up off the beach you can soon find yourself navigating around sand drifts that require some serious handling skills. Sand and bikes rarely mix, and when they do it can be a recipe for disaster.

Surviving the tight roads and hairpin turns the other battle is the wind and negotiating its direction and force. You can read the forecast all you like, but it's pointless. Being exposed on the coast means it's windy, all of the time, in every direction known to wind.

With tired legs and a smile on my face, I made it back to the Air B&B at a decent time. There's a sandwich waiting for me and an eager beaver ready for a day of exploring. It made sense to head back out to where I had just cycled. The scenery was undeniably beautiful and there were plenty of beaches to explore further and rest.

Day two of Tenby was more of the same, an early morning wakeup call by the seagulls, and on to the bike for some more cycling, but this time with more hills and a slight hangover. It didn't take long to sweat out the local Tenby ale as the inclines met me straight away, and the more I followed my GPS and headed north to Narberth the hills kept coming. If I was going to get around this Ironman course later in the year, I needed to deal with relentless hill climbs; this ride was just a taster.

The two notable inclines have names; you know they mean business when they have monikers and a reputation. After reaching Narberth and refueling it was time to hit the first big climb – Wisemans Bridge.

I'm a firm believer in that knowing what's around the corner is half the battle, no chance on this hill.

The overgrown tree lined sides create a canopy over the road, making it damp and littered with debris, it's a nightmare where you are clipped into your pedals and your rear wheel is spinning out from underneath you as you twist up and up. It is willpower alone getting you up there, in comparison to some of the other climbs on the route it's short and sharp, but I finally get up there through gritted teeth. I take some assurance now knowing it is do-able, but after 60 miles and again at 105 miles during Ironman, I'll need to find something else in the tank. What goes up must come down and I made sure I enjoyed the freewheeling downwards towards the beach.

Heartbreak Hill is next; this is a tasty climb as you spend the first section twisting up out of Saundersfoot, only then for the gradient to relax but continue for more that you'd like.

These "climbs" paled insignificant in comparison to what the pro's were probably used to, but they were my Alpe d'Huez and my Muro di Sormano. It took a fair bit of effort getting to the top of these, but I was getting great exposure and knowledge in what was required come race day.

Saundersfoot back into Tenby was like floating on a cloud, it's a smooth descent back to the B&B with hardly any need to pedal. More sandwiches and adventures awaited, I was just a bit tired after

25 miles and 2400ft of elevation gain. The weekend ended perfectly with some more downtime at the beach, and some active recovery walking some coastal paths. Who needs Canada, ay?

No time to rest, the second Sleep When You're Dead sprint distance triathlon held on Barry Island was up next and the first opportunity of the year to put into practice my open water sea swimming at race pace and to push the new aero bike.

Nothing had changed in terms of my gear, the wetsuit was holding together alright, it had a few snags which I managed to botch repair, but it was doing the job and I couldn't warrant a new wetsuit. My goggles did however need replacing, after being pulled in and out of my swim bag they were getting a bit scratched and blurry. Not a real problem in the pool, but in open water they were proving an issue. I replaced them like for like with the same make and model.

The objective of this race was to enjoy it and not put any pressure on myself. Turns out that is an effective race strategy.

The swim was strong, I managed to negotiate the current, waves and dodged other swimmers successfully, and I was out and on my bike within 20 minutes. I was pleasantly surprised but the transition area was a lot closer than previous year. Regardless, I took the small win.

The cycle, unlike last year, was two smaller loops closer to the start/finish line. This meant I was able to pace the first loop, and know where to push on the second loop. As I said before, knowing what is coming up is always half the battle. Getting off the bike in less than 40 minutes was another win for me, I was happy with that. I felt on course to bag a decent time. The run however was a struggle. Three loops of traversing up and down a big hill wasn't expected or really prepared for. Everyone runs the same route, so it's all relative. For me it was the undoing of me, reduced to a steady jog I was unable to settle my heart rate and breathing, the frequent adjusting of speed, incline and direction was tricky, but again, the same for everyone. I took the wake up call.

Crossing the finish line after a slightly disappointing 27 minute run, the race was completed with an overall time I was satisfied with considering I was making up the numbers and enjoying being part of the local event.

The journey home was typical debrief and performance analysing. Would I have been slower if I went all out, blowing up in exhaustion or was the nonchalance a factor in pacing the morning? My time would no doubt have been quicker on a flatter run course, but would that have placed me any higher in the finishers table? What I did notice was that the bike was aggressive, fast and impressive. Bottom line, I thoroughly enjoyed the morning, I engaged with a few other participants that I was still seeing around other events, and I ticked off the first triathlon of the year, onwards and upwards.

New to this year's plan was also active recovery. Previously I would have spent the remainder of the day sofa-bound, relaxing with my feet up, but by now, as a well seasoned amateur, I was aware of the benefits of active recovery. As much as your brain may need it, sitting still after a bout of activity for too long will prevent recovery, and with sleep providing ample amounts of rest I found that a short walk, some stretching or some futile attempts at yoga was hugely rewarding. It that meant that come Monday morning my body was already on the right path to building up the stress levels for the next push on training.

With 100 days until the biggest event of my life, it was safe to say that summer holidays spent lazing around a Mediterranean vista were nonexistent. However, with an understanding partner that is being pulled along on this triathlon journey you have to bend to some leniency. A weekend walking and taking in the sights of Lisbon was the plan. With my bike being too big for hand luggage, I resorted to packing my runners. I labeled that as a compromise.

Balancing a weekend break with some university friends and fitting in some training can be tricky, so the best time to run is normally early morning when everyone else is still sleeping. Alarm set for sunrise, I was ready.

Running north from the Praça do Comércio, up past Column of Pedro IV, through the Parque Eduardo VII and up to the Jardim Amália Rodrigues at around 08:00 is a great experience. The city is not quite alive yet, but it's warming up. Traffic is quiet but deliveries are beginning. The bakeries have been open a while, and the smell of the Pastel de Nada's serve an arousing level of temptation. From the top of Jardim Amália Rodrigues you're able to look back down towards the coast, banked either side by burnt orange tiled roofed buildings, castles and cathedrals. With the sun starting to pull some heat and light up the city below, it was a magical morning well spent. The day had begun, and with more exploring to be done I was able to relax and continue the sightseeing with a Pastel de Nata filled smug smile on my face.

That summer had also offered up a friend's wedding over in Ireland, conveniently sandwiched between the Cardiff triathlon and the SWYD triathlon events. Once again the runners were packed, and so too was my wetsuit. There was an opportunity to swim in the Atlantic Ocean as we were heading to Achill Island in County Mayo. Typically it was raining when we landed in Knock Airport but by the time we arrived into Achill, some 55 miles (95km) further west, we could have been mistaken for being somewhere more tropical. With the rain having moved on, the sun was shining bright and the invitation to swim in some of the clearest water I've ever seen was all too tempting, it didn't take me long to put on the wetsuit and get stuck in.

The runners came in handy too; they were used to help shake off one too many Guinness the morning after the wedding. Tell the people on your wedding table you're gearing up for an Ironman later that year, you'll find yourself drunker than planned.

There's something challenging about getting the aspiring athlete to loosen up and let their hair down. My training plan was purposely light for the weekend, so topping up my iron levels was a calculated risk I was prepared to take.

The month of June finished back on the start line for another dose of Olympic distance triathlon racing in Cardiff. This event was normally the main focus on my triathlon calendar; it was my home race and would commonly be the end goal. However, with Ironman being my "A" race this year, Cardiff was my "B" race. That meant all training and events were building up to Ironman in order to peak my physical fitness at the right time. I wanted to do well at the Cardiff Triathlon, but I saw it as more of a training session and also an opportunity to break in some new gear.

Impressively, after three years of open water swimming and triathlon events, my cheap entry level eBay purchased trisuit had reached the end of its life. The colour had faded and the white sections were now *off white.* The padding around the nether regions offered futile padding; it was time to move on. Ironman meant I would be wearing a trisuit for upwards of 17 hours, I needed it to last the wear and tear of 140 miles of swim, bike, run. I originally thought that opting for a specialist brand would break the bank, but to be fair, the price for something comfortable, smart and purpose built didn't add too much to how ever much this journey was costing. I was beyond counting the cost, out of total fear.

Back at the Cardiff triathlon, the event start was delayed due to an unforeseen incident on part of the bike route, nothing to with the triathlon but unfortunately there was a report of someone contemplating a jump from a bridge nearby. It was sobering moment; someone was in such desperate situation that they thought the only way out was suicide. We were at separate ends of the spectrum of perceivable happiness. I was just about to spend the next few hours doing something I love and then head home to recover in front of the TV with little care. I couldn't begin to think how their day would pan out; I couldn't put myself in their shoes because it was all too easy to think that there must be a way out of whatever situation they are in.

I am not saying triathlon is the answer to the unimaginable series of events that lead to thinking there was only one way out of a problem, I can however vouch from personal experience that exercise and especially being able to swim, cycle and run has allowed me to occasionally switch off the outside world for an hour or so. Offering a distraction and a platform for mindfulness has often presented order, clarity and escape. Burying your head in the sand and ignoring your problems is itself problematic, but the positive power of physical exercise is scientifically proven in abundance. There have been countless stories that I have read and watched of individuals who have reignited their lives and rose from drug addictions, crime and prison, obesity and poor mental health to name just a few. A short run and shift in mentality can start a domino effect of positivity, and I am all for preaching that.

With that in mind, I pushed forward with what was in front of me, knowing I was in a privileged position to do what I loved, with the belief I could comfortably complete the event.

Not only was my own mentality and belief starting to shift, but it was the same for my parents and loved ones. Back in 2015 when I first dipped my toe into triathlon, my parents basically thought I was crazy, and they weren't alone, even I believed it! However, a lesson I took far too long to learn was that in reality what the naysayers were really saying was that *they* couldn't do it, so therefore *I* was crazy for trying.

Others will put themselves in your position, and that's normal, but as soon as I understood where this negativity was coming from, it didn't matter what others thought. I understood the minimal amount of training needed to complete the challenges without getting into any difficulty. It sounds dramatic but in most of these events, it was me versus me. That narrative changed over the years, and whereas my mother would have been on the side lines praying I'd be alright and cheering me across the finish line, nowadays she would say good luck and let me know how you get on, all via text! That was alright, it reinforced my own belief.

The swim went as expected, I was a seasoned veteran of swimming in the waters of Cardiff Bay and I could confidently hold my own, keep it steady and avoid any discomfort. For the first time I wasn't overtaken by the following wave, a personal best. Swim time – 32 minutes.

Out of the swim and on to the bike my transition was a bit more focused, but I was still in no rush. The effort of cycling was steady and strong; however with the cycle route now made short due to the aforementioned incident, it meant counting six small laps of the route instead of three bigger loops I had prepared for. Remembering your lap number is more difficult than I thought, fortunately I had my pal Ronnie who was a lap ahead, confirming the number each time we passed in the opposite direction, providing me with a backup should I forget how to count to six. Cycle time – 55 minutes.

The 10k run was steady, controlled, and I only picked up the pace rounding the last corner of the Wales Millennium Centre. Crossing the line with a trademark sprint finish, straight to the bar with a medal around my neck, job done. Run time – 44 minutes.

Dissecting the stats later that afternoon it was clear something was amiss. The swim was quicker than the previous year, but I put that down to simply being a better swimmer. I had put in the work for my weakest discipline and it was evidently paying off, swimming was becoming my strength.

The cycle and run were also personal bests, but the recorded distances were noticeably shorter than what would be expected for an Olympic distance. This event is part of the Welsh Triathlon series, and you would expect the course to be measured precisely. Ultimately we are all racing the same route, so in terms of finish positions it's all relative. Personally I don't count the finish stats of this iteration of the event as correct, and I'm alright with that. A sub 45 minute 10k would be nice, but I'll wait. My "B race" proved everything it needed, and that was race exposure and a big training session towards Ironman Wales. I was on target with only a jellyfish infested hurdle to overcome. Shit was getting real, fast.

It was back to Tenby in July, a place definitely becoming my second home, and I couldn't complain. Once again Tenby was on full show, and this time I was part of it, right in the mix of triathlete enthusiasts. The Long Course Weekend has been running for a number of years, and was getting bigger and better each time. The most challenging iteration of this event stretches the commonly known distances familiar with Ironman of swim, bike and run, over Friday, Saturday and Sunday respectively.

The event also includes shorter disciplines to attract more entries; that means Tenby is once again full to capacity. Two months out from Ironman Wales, this is a great chance to get accustomed to race like conditions. Admittedly it is easier to replicate the bike and run route in and around Pembrokeshire, but being able to safely swim 2.4 miles in the same stretch of water to Ironman Wales is a perfect opportunity to benchmark your ability. Although some slight differences – this took part in the evening, so extra consideration had to be made for fueling and end of day fatigue. Not much was done leading to the start time and I ate a light lunch and some porridge an hour before the swim. I was winging it.

Being part of 2000 people running towards a jellyfish infested sea at 19:00 on a Friday evening was one of the most surreal moments of my life. There was music pumping and the sun was slowing setting, it was all quite magical. No time for a show, the open water waited. You may have been positioned on the beach according to perceived ability, but it was absolute carnage entering that water! Even the ones who held back to avoid the initial rush were embroiled in what seemed like an ambush on the sea, and I must admit I loved it.

Everyone was friendly on the beach, the camaraderie I was used to was present and correct, swimming is generally the most feared of the disciplines and there is a strange sort of comfort knowing we are all in the same boat. As soon as the hooter goes and the fireworks sound, it's all for one. Fear, anxiety and adrenaline mix and result in looking after number one.

I refuse to believe anyone in the water is out to purposely harm any other swimmer, but with arms and legs swinging and kicking in every direction in a condensed space, it was inevitable that one stray hand or foot would connect with another swimmer. I was punched and kicked, but I was inadvertently doing the same thing until the pack thinned out. There is not much you can do at this stage, other than just keep swimming.

After battling against the current and other swimmers, the next challenge reared itself in the first right hand turn buoy, or should I say bottle neck. This converted front crawlers into a pinch point of breast strokers and doggy paddlers, cue for more arms and legs landing on the faces and bodies of other swimmers. Nothing intentional, by now we all wanted to get out of the water, and it wasn't anyone's fault. Not only were we battling the act of swimming 2.4 miles with hundreds of other people, but we were sharing the water with wildlife, and in particular Barrel Jellyfish!

As it was the beginning of summer, the warm, clear water attracted a healthy number of well fed jellyfish, and we were in their water. The first time you see a jellyfish when swimming is met with exactly the reaction of when you see your last. They are frighteningly beautiful creatures, and for me, it was fear. I can honestly say that with every minute of that swim I must have seen about two jellyfish. Some appeared below me, some appeared on the side of me and others on top of the water ahead of me. When you didn't see a jellyfish you stressed over the next time you would, and then you did. Quite often during that swim you could see swimmers change direction abruptly or even hear the shouting of seeing one closer that they'd like.

Ever licked a battery as a kid? Being stung by a Barrel Jellyfish is pretty similar, a sharp zap which hits you and disappears almost instantly. Relatively harmless, but you would still rather avoid being stung and get out of the jellyfish soup as quickly as possible.

After the melee of the first turn, the route directed the swimmers parallel to the beach and that allowed for the pace to pick up as the tide provided assistance. The return stretch to the beach blinded most swimmers with clear goggles as the sun was setting just behind the alternatively painted sea front town houses. It was beautiful, but a bit of a nuisance as it meant dealing with another issue.

With wobbly legs the first loop was done and the "Australian" exit offered time to catch your breath and ready yourself for round two as you had it all to do again. By this time I was over the jellyfish, over the turn buoy bottlenecks and kicks to the face and I was just keen to get this swim wrapped up. Another 40 minutes later and I was running through the sand towards the finish line with a massive smile on my face. Relieved it was over, impressed that I had survived the swim and completed it within the 2 hour cut off time but more grateful that I managed to avoid being stung in the face.

Swim time – 1 hour 23 minutes, and around 166 jellyfish.

Back on terra firma, I drank a nonalcoholic beer and laughed with the other swimmers, we were all friends again, no hard feelings. The general consensus was that it was tough, but not the swim itself, more so the additional challenges. The sea was still, with no chop or strong currents to battle. What made it tricky was the amount of swimmers in the water, and also wildlife adding to the mix. On the whole, the atmosphere of the event was electric, which might have had something to do with the amount of jellyfish. It honestly felt like we were all in it together and what we had achieved was truly epic.

The swim was the start of a long weekend for a lot of the people on that beach, the following day most of the swimmers had a 112 mile cycle to complete and would cap it all off with a marathon on the Sunday morning. Some say the Long Course Weekend is tougher than an Ironman. The course is moderately the same, but the time in between each day allows your body to start recovering, but not fully, because you're either back on the bike or out on the marathon.

For me, the aim of the weekend was to bank that swim, and that was in the bag. For a change we decided to stay outside of Tenby and head further west for a weekend in St David's. We spent a few days exploring the beautiful coast, taking in the amazing scenery and a spot of swimming. I managed a gentle run and mapped out the plan for the next event, it was one I hadn't attempted before. Swimrun!

In the meantime the sessions on Training Peaks were getting heavier week by week, and although the loads were progressive, they were still taking a stress on my body. It was recommended that I visit a sports therapist and receive a sports massage. My girlfriend was on the case and found someone with a high rating nearby, offering a discount via a voucher website I was booked in with no fuss.

Arriving hot and sweaty in my shorts and T-shirt after a brisk cycle to the clinic, I filled out a health and safety form and I was soon up on a medical bed being bent in ways I wasn't too comfortable with.

Using a range on apparatus he was able to measure the acute angles of my raised legs, and it wasn't pretty. Hamstrings were tight, quadriceps were tight, calves were tight, my back was tight, shoulders were tight. Basically I was a walking talking ball of muscle knot and I probably shouldn't have left it so long before having a once over. With the hour session ticking away and so much ground to cover, the expert worked solely on my quads and hamstrings. Either he hated me or the pain was reflective of how tight my muscles were. Holding my breath to prevent shouting, he ran his thumbs, forcibly up and down stretches of muscle and tendons that made my eyes water, this went on for far too long.

As I left, exhausted, wobbling out on both legs I was assured that the pain was necessary and acted as a reminder that I should stretch and roll more often than I claimed to be doing. The foam roller became an essential piece of recover kit that is worth its weight in gold.

In an effort to build my swimming ability further, Ron and I decided it would be a great idea to enter the inaugural *All or Nothing* swimrun event starting and finishing at Barry Island. I'm reluctant to use the word *race* as the closest to being competitive in this event was at the start line with the other 19 pairs of swimrunners.

Swimrun is the brainchild of some drunken Swedish lads, bored and looking for a challenge. It basically involves swimming and running in and around a coastal region spanning a set distance. To speed up transitions between running and swimming, it's common practice to wear a wetsuit you're able to run in, and running shoes you are able to swim in. You wear it all for the duration. Oh, and this race is done in pairs, and you're normally tethered together by a 10m bungee cord. Bungee cord was optional in this race, but it was advised to stick close to your partner as you had to log your progress at multiple stages.

In hindsight this event was ill timed and totally unnecessary, my swimming was as strong as it was going to get and I was satisfied with my running. Combining the two was merely something fun to do, an opportunity to be part of a local event that's a little different. What was the worst that could happen?

With that in mind, my swimrun partner and I, wearing matching short sleeved wetsuits headed off for a mini adventure, running into the sea wearing some old running trainers and a nervous smile on our faces. Instantly noticing how the swimrun specific wetsuit comes into its own, offering buoyancy and flexibility in the right places, drying quickly after a swim it offered breathability during the run.

Swimming and running, in and out of the sea for 4 hours, for nearly 12 miles on one of the hottest days of the summer was a Sunday I really wasn't prepared for. The constant taste of salt, be it from the sea or sweat from our faces ensured we were both constantly thirsty, making the most of every water stop which to be fair were frequent. Running in wet and sandy trainers only encourages blisters that swell, burst and return the more you continue. The only remedy to alleviate the pain half way through an event is to stop whining and keep going. Words Ron frequently repeated towards my direction.

The alternating disciplines were also a nightmare for trying to steady my heart rate, forgetting how rugged the coastal path was with the inclines, the running was deadly, and the swim sections got challenging as the morning went on. It was an interesting training session and if anything I built a shit load of mental resilience. The majority of that came from the final swim leg. The changes in tide and current happen so quickly in this stretch of water, and windows of opportunity come in small pockets. By the time we reached the final swim leg of Whitmore Bay to Jacksons Bay, we were not in the desired window. You could say the complete opposite.

Digging deep and scraping the bottom of the energy tank we slowly, but surely made our way around Nell's Point, head on against the current. We knew we were safe as the volunteers were close on stand up paddle boards and kayaks, they were watching our every move. We didn't have too much to worry about other than finding energy to keep swimming. Stopping to grab my breath and take a rest was dangerous, the longer I treaded water, the more I moved in the opposite direction. It was a true battle of wits, and still to this day one of the toughest swims of my life, one I won't attempt again in a hurry, even if the tide *was* in my favour.

We managed to cross the finish line last but one, with some scrapes, blisters and tired bodies but each with a great big smile on our faces. Taking part in something new and different was the plan and we walked away with some great memories, or nightmares. Depending on which way we look at it.

No more events for fun, it was time to focus, Ironman was fast approaching.

Back Home

There were still a few weekends left until the training started to taper and with another golden opportunity to chuck the bike in the back of the car and make the 100 mile trip west to Tenby again was all too tempting to resist.

Coincidently, the chosen weekend fell in line with the peak of my training load. The plan was a 6 hour ride with an hour run straight after. This was the biggest brick session I would have attempted, and being the end of August, it was the hottest.

Loaded with fluid and snacks, I converted the planned cycling time and location into completing the "Big Loop" of the Ironman Wales route. This involved a cycle out to Angle, as previously ticked off and then a slight shift north to Narberth, on similar roads to what I had experienced on a previous visit. Aware of the "cut off" time during Ironman, I was keen to get this wrapped up in under 5 hours, as that's what I'd have to do on the day.

It all went to plan, the ride out to Angle through the lanes, passed the army barracks and through the sandy roads back to Pembroke were lovely. The wind was on my side and I found many opportunities to tuck into an aero position to make the most of the elements.

Reaching Narberth came at the right time, with the sun beaming down I was getting through my fluids quicker than anticipated. I knew that wouldn't be an issue on the day as there were plenty of feed stations along the route, but today, with the heat, I had barely enough to make it to the Narberth checkpoint.

From Narberth I knew what was coming, and I was ready. Conserving energy early on proved useful and with the increased levels of fitness and previous knowledge, I ascended both Wisemans Bridge and Heartbreak Hill easier than previously experienced. Don't get me wrong, they were still attacked painfully slowly, but I felt stronger and a lot more comfortable.

Descending back into Tenby I checked my onboard Garmin computer, it registered 4 hour 30 minutes. That was a big win for me, a confidence boost going into taper, knowing the next time I was on that cycle I *knew* I could make the cut off. I gave myself no excuses.

I was however exhausted, and with an hour run still yet to do I decided to call it a day on the bike, park it in the Air B&B and lace up my runners for a 6 mile run of the Ironman route.

By the time I got back out it was midday and the sun was an issue. Salts and sugars were seriously depleted and fatigue was kicking in. Frustratingly and potentially dangerous, the run route on any normal day isn't as pedestrian friendly as one would hope. The run takes you back up the road out of Tenby that I had just cycled down. With the pavements disappearing, you're forced to either run on the road or the grass verge, both as problematic as the other. Opting for a mixture, I was able to plod up the inclines and maintain a steady speed on the declines, averaging a decent 9 minute/mile pace I banked 6 miles in under an hour. I was done.

Taking a dip in the sea later that day it dawned on me that the peak of my training was complete. I had put in some serious work in the pool most mornings, I had clocked the full distance both inside and in open water environments. Mixing up the distance and efforts on the bike most weekends and pounding the pavements with brick sessions and half marathons. I had done all I could.

Now with twenty days until I faced the Dragon, the load reduced and kept to an "easy" pace. The rationale behind this being that with the bulk of my efforts banked, I would experience a trimmed down training load in preparation for peaking on race day.

The hard part was done, the training was complete and I tried to see Ironman as the biggest training session of them all, it was no way viewed as a race. My body was ready and I just wanted to complete it in one piece. By now the problem wasn't my body, it was my head.

Life threw a curveball at the end of August and I found myself made redundant and changing jobs in a new city. I was reluctant from the start, and I found early on that I wasn't the right fit for the new company, and that was fine. Hindsight is a wonderful look back into the past, and configured to our own bias. The new job was offered on a plate and with Ironman clouding my vision, I blindly accepted it. Within a few weeks I knew it was just a stepping stone and grinded out the earlier, longer commutes and disengagement. Not my finest hour, but Ironman was consuming so much of me, and after all the training I had put in, I put Ironman before my career. I accepted that.

Fortunately it was taper season, and my training plan was purposely reduced in effort, which worked hand in hand with having to start work earlier, further away.

This extra commute time meant I had more time to think about Ironman, and exhaustingly everything that could go wrong. Nerves were natural, but worrying about complicated swims, bike mechanicals or injuries were circulating my head, constantly.

What helped was speaking to my coach, who was now inevitably a good friend and confidant. After spending the best part of 12 months working closely together, he knew just what to say. Confident in my ability and with full belief he didn't need to reassure me of my performance. Regarding my mindset he made it clear and simple. He pleaded for me to not worry about everything and only concentrate on what I could control. Thinking about a million and one external factors that could hamper the day is wasted energy and more importantly I could miss the opportunity to think about something that *was* in my control. One thing I didn't need to worry about was the weather, even though the weather app was the most frequently accessed feature of my phone, I wasn't new to cycling in wind and rain. I just preferred it to stay dry, we all did.

With my ability not in question, I adopted the new mindset that I just need to be present and deal with one of the million external factors that may face me on the day.

Saying that, thinking about every piece of triathlon item needed for the big day was a headache in itself. I needed some lists, and that meant a list of lists. By the time I set off for Tenby for the last time as an Ironman wannabe, I had flow charts, diagrams, instructions to my future self and the Magna Carta of lists.

Dance with the Dragon

Driving to Tenby on the Friday afternoon, with two sleeps to go the excitement was building, but I tried to stay calm and not get carried away. I was already checking out the bikes attached to cars heading the same way down the M4 and wondered if the passengers were exceed as I was. We arrive and after unloading all the gear into the Airbnb that was situated on the actual run route, I skipped straight off to registration, via the strategically positioned merchandise tent.

A little light in the wallet, with an Ironman bag full of fate tempting merchandise, I completed the mind boggling registration. The instructions were thorough and I left with some wristbands, a T1 bag, a T2 bag, a *bike* special requirements bag, a *run* special requirements bag, a white bag for after the race and that oh-so-famous pink bag! Of all bags in my possession, the pink bag was the Holy Grail. This unassuming pink plastic bag was to be hung on numbered pegs that zig zagged the swim exit from the beach to the streets above. What you put in the bag was totally up to you. I planned for an electrolyte drink to replenish salts and sugars, a bottle of water to wash my feet of sand, some older running trainers and a banana. It also provided an option to carry the wetsuit should I decide to strip down to my trisuit. The only rules at this point; do not be naked, and do not leave your pink bag behind. Leaving the bag would be classed as littering and you would be faced with disqualification. To this day I still have that pink bag, not sure when I can dispose of it in fear of a belated DQ.

Now with so many bags and instructions that I failed to write down, I didn't have time to stress over what goes where and by when. It was off to the race briefing for more instructions to fit into my busy brain.

Nerves, excitement and an insane amount of fit people filled the local Pavilion for the race briefing. It was easy to identify the first timers from the people who knew what they were doing. Not only because of the orange bands on the wrists of the Virgins, but also by the confidence some people carried. It was at this point I knew that I had signed up for something bigger than I originally thought. I'm just enjoying the ride and looking to finish, but there were potential winners in this room, professionals, semi-professionals and age groupers pushing for Kona qualification.

The race briefing was a mixture of rules, do's and don'ts. To be honest it was all a bit of a blur but I remembered some main pointers - don't litter, don't be a dick, don't forget your pink bag and do have fun, briefing done. After some food and strangely the only beer of the weekend, it was time to call it a day. Getting back to the B&B I didn't bother with organising any of the transition bags that evening, the room looked upside down with all my event gear but an early night was needed for an early Saturday morning start.

With my bike and two of the many bags needing to be parked and hung by 15:00 that afternoon, there was plenty of time to enjoy a Saturday morning sunrise and it was the perfect opportunity to mimic race day morning. Up at 05:00 to eat some porridge (which by now I could stomach after prepping early feeds all week), I took on some fluids and got down to the beach for a 07:00 swim. I was staying a big stone's throw away from the water's edge, so it was ideal. A lot of people had the same idea. I managed about 2000m of gentle swimming which calmed some nerves; the sea was a bit choppy but no cause for concern and zero sight of jellyfish. Fuelling and hydration seemed to work well and the thought of swimming another 1800m seemed achievable. The weather was also looking promising and scheduled to remain dry; all that time spent checking the forecast every hour during the week leading up to the weekend was wasted. I ignored the wind speed and direction, as I have experienced, it's always windy out on the coast.

The next big thing on the list was to drop off the transition bags and rack my bike. This filled me with absolute dread. Mainly because if you didn't have your bike and bags racked and stowed by 15:00, it would be very difficult to do so afterwards, they were the rules. After meticulously sorting, arranging and rearranging the several bags, ticking off lists upon lists it was time to make my way across to the transition area.

Taking a picture of all my transition bag items in a pile before putting them in the individual transition bags proved a smart move. I was able to look back at the pictures and settle any anxiety should I forget what I had packed after the transition area was closed.

The bike transition area was pretty much a car park full of bikes that cost more than all of my worldly possessions. But that's triathlon. My bike area was in line with a car park light and a couple of bikes in from the end of a row. After a few dummy runs of finding my bike and transition area from both the bike out and bike in routes I was confident in finding my location on race day. I left my bike overnight, praying it was still there at 06:00 Sunday morning.

My bags were hung in the huge tent on numbered pegs in the transition area, separate to where my bike was stationed. As every bag looked the same it was vital you remembered your number. Alternatively you could check the race tattoo on your arm.

Bike racked, bags dropped and at 14:00 the Ironkid events were well underway by this point. Hundreds of kids of different ages gearing up to be the next generation of Ironman adorned the town walls of Tenby. It was pretty inspiring stuff seeing youngsters running around the streets, wearing bib numbers and finishing at the Ironman arch. I purposely avoided going anywhere near the finish line and red carpet. I only wanted to see it one time, and that was to be the next day, after 140.6 miles of moving forward.

With time running out before I wee in my wetsuit on a beach surrounded by 2000 others pretty much doing the same thing, panic strikes! With the inevitable occurrence that my Ironman race will roll well into the night, it dawned on me that it would more than likely get a bit chilly running around in a one piece that leaves little to the imagination. Not having brought a suitable t-shirt to Tenby, it was back to the merchandise store for another Ironman branded purchase. This was to go into my Special requirements run bag, which is luckily handed to a man in a van the morning of the race.

Time to relax, I meet up with some friends and family and force down some food, maybe the last supper. Surrounded by positive energy the conversations were on a complete opposite side of the spectrum compared to the conversations I had back in 2016 when taken part in my first triathlon. My parents, although nervous, totally believed in my ability to finish the race. Whereas before, these loved ones thought I was absolutely crazy, now saw the benefits of the journey I had been on. "You got this, don't be shit", was pretty much the parting words when I waved them goodbye that evening, hoping the next time I'd see them I would be well on my way to becoming an Ironman.

The night was drawing in and I was still trying to find solace with the thoughts racing around my head and with that I decided to attend Ironprayer, it was perfectly scheduled for the right time. I wouldn't say I'm a religious person, but I do have a respect and appreciation for nature, the earth and our position on this planet. Call that spiritual if you may. Ironprayer was the "non-denominational" labeled, but a clearly Christian orientated space to enjoy some words of encouragement, share some stories and enjoy some quiet time. Basically, if you're feeling like you'll drown in the sea, bonk on the bike or shit yourself on the run; this was the time to put those perfectly rational thoughts to bed. It really did help settle those last nerves, I was ready.

Relaxed, prepped and ready to face the Dragon, 21:00 came around and it was time for some sleep. My Ironman itinerary reading was done for the last time, my kit was laid out for the morning, I turned my phone off, kissed my girlfriend good night and closed my eyes for what I thought would be a restless eight hours of night terrors and sweats.

Alarm went off at 05:00, I slept like a baby.

Sticking to the tried and tested plan I eat a bowl of porridge, a banana, take on water, salts and sugar. With an energy gel planned for an hour before kickoff, I calculated it should be enough to see me to the first transition, this was an oversight. It wasn't enough.

With 90 minutes to spare, I palm off the special requirement bags to a man in a van, hoping I have enough emergency supplies of bike components, snacks, painkillers, plasters, salt tablets and sugar. I check on the bike, carry out some last minute I-have-no-idea-what-I'm-doing mechanical checks, load my water bottles and secure my Garmin on board computer praying the battery lasts. Because if it's not on Strava, it doesn't count right?

Back to the B&B for another nervous poo, I put on my trisuit, pull on my wetsuit, stick on my old (transition) runners, take my pink bag and head towards the beach.

It's a strange walk to the beach, it's 06:30 in the morning, it's still dark but eerily not cold. It's because the streets are jam packed full of racers and supporters adding body heat to the streets, genuinely wishing everyone a safe day out there.

I kiss my girlfriend goodbye and wipe the tears from her eyes. She knew how much this meant to me, and as invested from the start, she would be praying every minute from the start to the finish.

I make my way down the zig zag ramp towards the beach and pegged my pink bag at the allocated number. Reaching the beach the racers were asked to self seed according to expected swim time. I opted for the 1 hour 30 minute swim pen. I knew I could swim it faster, but I felt comfort knowing I was under-selling myself and not getting carried away. After all the events I had completed and achieved, there was still an element of doubt and lack of confidence.

The mood is a mixture of all sorts of emotions and the wait on the beach is equally as intense. There are last minute adjustments to goggles, wetsuit straps, zips and sports watches. There were people stretching, talking, praying, warming up in preparation for a long day. No one in deep conversation, mainly just small talk and well wishes. The focus was on the day, regardless of how fit and fast you were, what lay ahead was one of the biggest challenges on the Ironman circuit, and it was moments away.

All set but the Welsh National Anthem to be belted out, a spine tingling rendition…

"Gwlad, gwlad, pleidiol wyf i'm gwlad.
Tra môr yn fur i'r bur hoff bau,
O bydded i'r hen iaith barhau."

A gun sounds, followed by a roar of supporters with hooters and horns. Fireworks exploded overhead and any pre race trance was rudely disturbed. Heart rate pounding, we wait a moment before our pen is released and then charge towards the water, ready for battle.

It's go time!

I reiterate the plan out loud; "no need to run, take your time, flush your wetsuit, acclimatise, steady your nerves, get your head down and just. Keep. Swimming!". As expected and previously experienced, it was a bit of a mess at the early stages, the washing machine was in full cycle, and for the first 5 minutes there were arms and legs everywhere. This is where your bottle can go and make those 2.4 miles a total nightmare. I kept calm, steadied my breathing and using slightly faster swimmers ahead of me I was able to ride their wake and reduce energy exertion. Other than staying on course and sighting, the next challenge was navigating the first turn buoy to what becomes that fist fight bottleneck. Within 20 meters of the first turn buoy, some 800m into the swim, there are multiple channels of swimmers dramatically adjusting their course to bank around this buoy. Once again, front crawl changes to breaststroke and whether you like it or not, you're caught up in the melee. Surviving with no issues there was one more not-so-busy right hand turn and it was a swim back to the beach for the Australian exit in readiness for the second loop.

First lap done and now to execute the Aussie exit plan. Take your time, no need to run and DO NOT TAKE OFF YOUR GOGGLES, a lesson I learnt from the Long Course Weekend swim a few weeks previous. Starting the second loop it wasn't as congested, no washing machine spin cycle to deal with, but the first turn buoy was looking the same as before. This time I changed my tactics and hung further left to swoop right around the pile up in sheer perfection.

With the back of the swim broken, the end of this leg was insight. My body was feeling alright but hunger was looming. Managing to get through the swim with no major issues in a time of 1 hour 19 minutes, I was very pleased with that. By now the spectator numbers had grown and it is impossible to not feel overwhelmed while crawling out of that sea. All I needed to do now was find my bag and ready myself for T1, and with 100's of other people doing the same thing it was pretty busy, but everyone was in a great mood.

I decided to strip my wetsuit down to my waist, wash my feet of sand, stick on my old runners, and take my time walking the long road to the bike. I was pretty hungry by this point so running this transition while eating a banana would not have ended well. I enjoyed the walk, took in the atmosphere and waved to friends and family. Only a year ago I was part of the crowd cheering on racers, and now I was being cheered, such a surreal moment. This won't be the last time I'll say this but the crowds were absolutely incredible!

Swim time 1 hour 19 minutes (zero jellyfish)

The plan was to be out on the bike by 09:00, by the time I got to the transition area I had about 15 minutes to fully remove my wetsuit, dry off in the tent, consume the liquid and food I needed and more important than anything else, was to make myself comfortable. I am notorious for taking my time during transitions, but with Ironman it was pointless rushing through the first transition and forgetting something that would make the majority of the day even more hard work.

I found my bike ready and waiting with no issues, I was out of T1 with time to spare, now to face 7 hours of cycling the unforgiving hills of Pembrokeshire which after spending a fair portion of the summer practicing on, I knew what was to come and I knew they would be brutal.

The first goal on the bike ride was to make the first cut off; this was about 70 miles into the route and also signified the completion of the "Big Loop". With this in mind I had to weigh up energy conservation and control my adrenaline. Easier said than done, because what happened is I went flat out, hammering the pedals, buzzing on excitement and consequently paid the price 50 miles in when the hills turned up.

10 miles in and I've settled into a number of cat and mouse games with the other riders who are of a similar fitness level. For the first 50 miles you

get used to seeing the same people in and around you. Sometimes you'll have a boost of energy and overtake some riders; other times those same riders will overtake you. There is a "no drafting policy" in place, but sticking to this is nigh on impossible. The only practical way of abiding by this is to just cycle, and avoid blatantly tucking in and sitting on someone's rear wheel.

What also becomes apparent is that because Ironman has closed off all of the roads, there is not much the local residents can do other than embrace it. So it seems that all neighbours get together and set up their camp to cheer, holla and whoop at the riders flying by. Young, old, fancy dressed, dancers, singers, drummers, you become accustomed to what you see. They all showed up. I'm not sure how much they know, but it helps every single rider. They are such a boost. I knew this well before noon and the party was about to begin.

Freshwater West was next, I understood from experience that this section was sketchy, but unfortunately not everyone knew this. Impossible to keep the area clear, the wind had kicked up enough sand to cause an issue. Unfortunately someone had come off at this point and emergency services were already on the scene, with the rider being attended to. The road being only wide enough for one vehicle meant the race was held up for 15 minutes as riders had to dismount and walk through the sand, up over the bank and around the ambulance.

By chance, this allowed for a slight rest before a tough climb out of the area.

The cycle route takes you to Angle where you meet your first bunch of amazing volunteers at the feed stations, and then back out through Pembroke town, where by now the bars are open and the locals are starting to sample the home brew. The party has now started and it's a lovely distraction.

The hills come next, one on top of the other. Through lanes and the back of beyond, the locals are still out making themselves known. You bottle the encouragement and keep pushing on. Knowing you'll be back around in a few hours for the smaller loop.

Climbing into Narberth was a painful experience, but the town had transformed into something that looked like a carnival. The riders were greeted by a karaoke King of Pop belting out some classics over a sound system and the locals were dancing, singing and cheering on the riders. The scenes were unbelievable and another welcomed distraction.

Through another feed station to replenish the fluids and grab some energy gels and on to two of the notorious climbs – Wisemans Bridge and Heartbreak Hill in Saundersfoot. I knew what to expect, I was experienced with the route, but I still had to climb them again. With each push of the pedals I kept on going and I didn't stop. It's difficult to have any other thought in your mind other than just get to the top. The Wisemans bridge climb I was cheered up by a large contingent of supporters in fancy dress, and Heartbreak Hill was more like Alpe d'Huez, Tour de France style with the cheering crowds lining the road allowing for just enough room for two bikes side by side.

Hearing a louder roar than normal I managed to spot my old friend Tom who was staying nearby. He had gathered a few friends who purposely positioned themselves to give me a much needed boost of energy, and it worked. My mind instantly returned to the first day out on a road bike with him, I had come such a long way. It was a truly spine tingling climb, one to remember for sure, and I had to do it all again shortly after.

At the top of Heartbreak Hill was the special requirements bag that I had packed with a pick and mix of what I thought I would want at this stage of the Ironman. It was a tough call; being a chocoholic I thought a few bars would be perfect, but typically and not surprisingly I was craving crisps. After refilling some pockets and bottles I was heading back towards Tenby to tick off the big loop and head out for the second loop.

Being part of the crowd supporting the previous year, I knew my girlfriend would be at the same vantage point as last year ready to cheer me on at the intersection. After 70 miles and without fail I heard the words of encouragement I needed, whizzing past I only had time to shout "I love you", and away up the road I continued. That was enough for the both of us. Within that brief moment we both knew we were alright.

The small loop was a bit of a slog. Legs were cramping and stiffening up in the climbs, I wasn't taking on enough salts and liquids as I should have, and time was ebbing away. Doubt started to creep in for the first time; but I was going as quickly as I could. Triathlon can be a lonely sport, but only if you want it to be. At this stage of the day those around me were all struggling, fatigue had hit and we were all up against the ropes. But we didn't come this far, to only come this far. Camaraderie kicked in and we were willing each other to just keep pushing and make the most of the surroundings.

The smaller climbs were getting tough at this stage but after every effort going up, I took the descents as respite to stretch out the body while standing out of the saddle. That also gave the undercarriage a little break, because by now it was in tatters.

Pushing on to Narberth, where the locals were still out raving, the support was unwavering. A general easy spin of the legs to the Wiseman's bridge and Heartbreak Hill climbs followed, which by now were a bit thin on the ground with supporters. They had understandably made their way to Tenby to continue their own marathon of a day.

After picking up a few more bits from the last feed station and special requirements bag it was pretty much downhill to Tenby, passing others who were already well into the run. The winner had already crossed the finish line by this point.

Cycle time - 7 hours 45 minutes.

I made it! The cycle was always going to be the majority of the day and as more things can go wrong on the bike I was relieved to dismount, I had made it and survived with no major issues. Now I knew I had about six hours to complete a marathon, and even though I was knackered and my legs didn't really work properly, I knew I could get around the four loops of the marathon, it was just a matter of how.

As much as I wanted to run the whole thing, my legs and stomach didn't allow for it. With four 10k laps to run, the last leg turns into a game of will and mental strength. The plan was to run while in the town during any flat sections, and then run depending on how I felt during any of the hill sections. Stopping wasn't really an option, but crossing that finish line before midnight was the only goal, the time was irrelevant. This was my first Ironman, my biggest personal challenge and crossing the finish line would be my personal best.

After switching off the near dead Garmin computer I gladly said goodbye to the bike, and headed into the transition tent to reissue my feet with a fresh pair of socks to stay as comfortable as possible.

Once again, best laid plans out of the window quite early on. Wanting to hit the ground running it actually took a while for me to get going. Trying to maintain a forward motion on foot was tough. Without too much detail, my body needed to use the loo, but it couldn't. My body needed one thing and my mind needed something else, or someone else. I needed to find my girlfriend and let her know how I was getting on. I was worrying about her, worrying about me.

It's easy to forget that friends and family are going through an equally stressful day. Granted they had not been swum over while swallowing salt water, climbing over 8000ft on the bike and running well on into the night. But they are constantly worrying, tracking, cheering and praying that nothing happens for long stretches of time without really knowing how their loved one is getting on.

After turning a few crowd lined corners I saw my girlfriend, crying. They were tears of joy as she had been following my progress on the Ironman tracker and knew the bike leg was out of the way. It was the bike discipline we were both silently worried about, but I still had a marathon to run. After a quick chat and update of where my mind and body were at, it was time to chip away at the 26 miles. I had come this far and the only way was forward.

The first loop was an interesting one. I was riding high after making it off the bike in one piece; yet I was concerned about the other riders still yet to come in. I was impressed by the runners who had already clocked a number of run laps and were still looking strong. I was looking anything but strong, but I was determined and kept a smile on my face and enjoyed the dying hours of the event.

The first loop also allowed me to get my bearings, work out where the milestones were, how soon the hills kicked in and any opportunities to take it easy. I was due to run four of these and getting comfortable with the surroundings helped a great deal. What I found reassuring about this first loop was that there were plenty of toilets, feed stations and volunteers ready to provide any help or assistance. You were never alone, the crowds and volunteers constantly kept you motivated. It would be a difficult day without each and every one of them, first one done.

Second loop swings around and it's now clear there was a long way to go. It was hard breaking it down into 10k laps, so I broke each lap down to manageable checkpoints and sights I enjoyed seeing on the first. There were feed stations, residents in front gardens and triathlon clubs situated at certain corners. The volunteers helped massively, giving out the next coloured wrist band to identify what lap the runners were on, each band received was like a power boost. There was a young boy on a set of drums, drumming a motivational beat on one of the hills and plenty of friends and family in the crowd. These checkpoints and stage gates were critical in maintaining focus and encouragement.

Physically, the second loop was equally as tough. The night was drawing in and the temperature was dropping. It was now I made the call to collect the t-shirt from the special requirements bag, I feel this could have been the difference between finishing the race or not. I count myself lucky having thought about the worst case scenario last minute. After spending some time in the toilet (mainly negotiating the stripping down of a tri-suit with a t-shirt on top) I felt I had a second wind. A bit lighter on my feet and warmer up top, I finished the second loop a lot more positive, but I ensured I didn't get ahead of myself. Half way is half way, you're so close but there is still so much more to do. Using the crowd as support to keep you moving, they were having a great time getting more drunk and lairy as the night moved on. Tenby was turned up to 11, the party was in full swing. You couldn't help but to keep on going.

The third lap was a battle of wits. The pro's were home and dry by now, what they put their body through is admirable. My body and mind were taking the hit. I had broken the back of the run and knew what was around each corner, whether that was a good thing or a bad thing. I still had time on my side and I was crossing that finish line on my hands and knees if I had too.

It was dark, I was cold, but the crowds were STILL on their feet cheering and shouting. The other runners around me shared the pain, and we were all digging deep. All the hard work, the early mornings, the long rides, the setbacks, the injuries, the commitment and sacrifices all come down to the last lap. I was doing this, and I was going to enjoy it!

Prior to race day I got chatting on social media to someone who was also taking part in the race, she had done a few before and knew what to expect. She told me that you only get to finish your *first* Ironman, once, so enjoy it.

So I did!

It was getting late into the night, but the atmosphere was still lively, and after making an effort to thank the crowds and volunteers, the red carpet beckoned and I was ready to join in the fun. Lined both sides with cheering supporters I took the time to absolutely milk the last few steps. Cheering, shouting, twirling and waving my arms around like a lunatic. Totally in a zone of pure euphoria I managed to miss sight of my parents, best friends and girlfriend. With one last shout of relief I jumped over the finish line under the infamous timing arch hearing the words that I never thought I would ever hear. "You are an Ironman!".

Run time 5 hours 50 minutes

I crossed the finish line in around 15 hours 30 minutes, I don't know for sure, it's not a stat I have bothered to remember, I just know that I crossed that finish line.

Hands on my knees, my body thankful that I had put a stop to this onslaught, I stand up with a medal around my neck. By a strange turn of coincidence, it was hung by the lady who I chatted to on instagram a few days prior. Laura Siddell, Pro triathlete, she finished third! Star struck and exhausted, we have a quick photo and I hobble off to the recovery tent for some pizza and to collect my belongings.

By now it was about 23:00, in total disbelief that in my own way I had tamed the dragon, I needed to see my family who were lost in the crowd. They were as equally knackered and after finding them and shedding a few tears the only thing I wanted to do was support some of the other finishers. Triathlon gear dropped back to the B&B I changed into some warm, clean clothes and headed back to the finish line to see the last runners across the line in what's called Heroes Hour. Some were leaving it pretty close to the midnight cut off but everyone who crossed that line gave it their all. It may have taken these finishers all day, but I respect anyone who completes an Ironman, whether they finish first, somewhere in the middle or at the very end. Everyone has a tough day out there.

 With my stomach all over the shop I didn't fancy the beer I thought I would have, I decided to take on more salts to help prevent any cramp in my come down.

 It was 01:00 and it was time for some rest, for both my girlfriend and I. Unable to sleep I lay in bed reviewing the main points of the day. The whole operation from start to finish ran like a well-oiled machine. The organisers, the volunteers, Tenby and Pembrokeshire, the health and safety crews, emergency services, and the supporters, they all get behind each and every racer and I was, and will be, forever grateful to be on the receiving end of that. I finally close my eyes, and cramp up.

My eyes reopen the next morning to the sound of Seagulls squawking and a body that felt broken in multiple places. A morning-after-the-night-before realisation that I didn't have to train for an Ironman was, and still is a strange feeling. It was done and dusted; the itch had well and truly been scratched. After coming to terms with what had happened the night before it was off to the nearest greasy spoon for a full veggie breakfast followed by one last credit card fuelled trip to the merchandise tent. At this stage I wasn't sure if I would ever complete another Ironman event again. The journey was long and I achieved a goal I never knew was possible. Unfortunately that meant spending more money on hoodies, t-shirts, coats, lanyards, mugs and whatever else that was emblazoned with the Ironman logo and the word "Finisher". I mean how much Ironman clobber can one person actually wear at one time? What's the rule? A hat, hoodie and a lanyard too much? There's only one way to find out. They were my final tokens to remember the weekend by, to be honest I had also run out of money!

We said goodbye to Tenby soon after, it had served us well through multiple visits and the small town in Pembrokeshire will be etched on my brain as a place full of great memories for a long long time.

Still tired and sore we ended our weekend with some relaxation and recuperation at St Brides Spa in Saundersfoot. Making full use of the steam room, sauna, Jacuzzi and beautiful infinity pool overlooking the bay, was a great ending. Getting home that Monday afternoon we unloaded the car and remained on the sofa digesting the whole weekend, Strava activities loaded, job done.

So that was it, Ironman 2019, with the support of my nearest and dearest I had completed it. When asked if I'd do another Ironman the initial response was no way, never again! The journey, which I feel I fully embraced, took over every aspect of my life. The time, the money, the early starts and grumpy afternoons, the setbacks and injuries, the tiredness in work, the stress to my body and more worryingly the impact on my personal relationship. Ironman encompassed my whole life, and others close to me.

…but when asked again a few months later, after over indulging and dropping training completely, my answer had changed. The honest answer is that I would love to do another one, but not yet. Training for an Ironman and being part of a community spanning 150 countries is something I was and am truly proud of. I'm just in no rush to do it all again, and to be fair, I wouldn't want to put my partner through it all again too. I wouldn't have crossed the start line, let alone the finish line without her; it was just as painful for her, just in many different ways.

For now, my Ironman days are over, the thought of training upwards of 15 hours per week and putting other areas of my life on hold just didn't appeal to me anymore, I am retired for the foreseeable future, but not from my triathlon days as a whole. I've drawn the line at getting an M-Dot tattoo on my calf, but I still have affection for triathlon, the love hasn't been lost and I couldn't imagine not swimming, cycling and running. With the Cardiff Triathlon being such a great event and close to home, it would be the only event I would continue in order to maintain some sort of physical benchmarking. I am also seeing an increase in triathlon engagement, with more events and groups popping up and with that I find myself in a position where I can share some wisdom, some do's and don'ts and still stay connected to a sport that isn't going anywhere other than forward.

Crossing the finish line at Ironman Wales 2019 had been the end of a 10 year journey that at times I didn't know I was on.

Life can serve strange coincidences and with my personal life changing direction in the form of redundancy and uncertainty, finishing Ironman brought on clarity and belief that I could achieve anything if I just believed in myself. The feeling of closure and the start of something new was overwhelming; a strong sense of a new beginning was coming and it was closure that came at the right time.

There was, of course, one more event to do! To bring my journey full circle I signed up for the British Heart Foundation 5k Santa Jog, revisiting this event 10 years later for the first time. What I loved about completing my full circle is that no one made a big deal about it, nobody cared, just me. It was the final hurrah, and it meant so much to me.

Both the 2009 Santa Jog and Ironman Wales 2019 medals sit side by side on a cabinet in full view, they are a constant reminder that for me, anything is possible.

I had also forgotten the Ironman money train will follow you around for a while. Not long after the dust had settled, out comes the email with a link to a shit load of watermarked photos, tempting you to relive the day in megapixels. THAT was in fact the last Ironman related purchase I made. An expensive album of photos stored on my computer as a digital reminder. Annoyingly they were discounted the following week too!

There is no Finish Line

As I write this, COVID-19 has ripped a hole right through our world. The way we live, work, socialise, rest and play has been turned upside down and understandably sport has been sidelined unless it's safe to host and be a part of, and rightly so.

Looking forward, whether we like it or not, the way triathletes travel the world and take part in events will never be the same again. The previously unquestionable nature of jumping on an aeroplane, a train or even driving 100 miles down the M4 to Tenby will now always have an element of considering safety. The thought of just standing next to someone on the beach ready to run into the sea and swim 2.4 miles seems unimaginable at present.

The frequent local lockdowns, stay at home orders and national restrictions on movement have forced a new way of training in truly creative ways. Professional athletes have had to think outside the box, adapt their training and come up with ways to maintain a competitive level of fitness. Social media channels gave us a front row seat to individuals clocking mileage in their homes and gardens, whether it was via indoor training bikes, treadmills, laps of the living room or even swimming in a garden pool, tethered by some bungee cord. Of course, with Captain Sir Tom Moore showing us determination in the face of adversity, did we have any excuse? I surely didn't. While I've not been able to mimic swimming in a two bed flat, I was inspired and managed to complete a number of personal "events" at home.

Cycling for 24 hours on an indoor turbo trainer seemed like a good idea at the time but it soon dawned on me that cycling non-stop through the night, with no sleep and only toilet breaks was a true test of will power. Between the saddle sores, nerve damage in my hands and the lack of sleep my mind and body went to some strange places. Familiar with digging deep, the sleep deprivation added hallucinations and life affirming questions. Mainly, you can achieve anything if you put your mind to it, it just comes down to – how badly do you want it?

Cycling 350 miles on an indoor trainer isn't the most appealing of challenges, but raising £1,000 for a children's charity added a level of accountability that I clearly use as a motivator during trying times.

More sleep depriving challenges followed but this time it involved a 24 hour marathon. The premise was actually quite simple: run just over a mile, every hour, for 24 hours. The challenge itself was downright devilish. Starting at midnight I was already awake past my bedtime, the mile took on average 10 minutes, so by the time I returned, stretched, ate and closed my eyes I was getting ready for the next hour to strike. Sleeping felt like blinking and eating was purely for fueling purposes. My body just didn't know what it was doing, and my mind was totally shattered. Finishing at 23:14 the following day made for a good few days of realigning my body clock.

Looking for further inspiration may come in the form of David Goggins. Goggins is an ex Navy SEAL, former Air Force Member, ultra-marathon runner, record holder, triathlete and all round bad ass who promotes a challenge that he occasionally eats for breakfast. It requires running four miles, every four hours, for 48 hours. This is some next level challenge that for me, requires some logistical planning but is on the horizon and ticks the box of being achievable, but for also being absolutely daft. With all the time spent building my body physically and time spent (as Goggins calls it) callusing my mind, I'm comfortable approaching this with the same intrigue as before – let's see what happens.

The last ten years of my life have seen interest in sports and physical activity taken to new levels, where my own limits have been pushed further and further. From running around the neighborhood block out of breath to running now most days in a variety of landscapes. The days of flapping dramatically in a swimming pool seem a million years ago as I can now comfortably hold my own during a busy sea swim, battling waves, currents and jellyfish. I've grown from having a less than a mild interest in anything outdoorsy to now looking for the next adventure and constantly chasing challenges. I no longer use Asthma as a hindrance, I have learned to live with it and keep it under control. I enjoy the outside, I enjoy pushing the limits and seeing what happens, and I do frequently wonder what more I could or would have achieved if I had the same level of sporting interest I do now, when I was a teenager. Hindsight is a bitch, and without that leap of faith we'll never know what we are capable of.

Back to triathlon and over the last 12 months I have seen sporting events being postponed and cancelled more times than I care to count. A triathlon race is seemingly a long way from materialising, but we have to stay positive, we didn't come this far too only come this far. The world will adapt as will triathlon and other sporting events, I am confident of that.

We must remind ourselves that the sport of triathlon transcends the actions of just swimming, cycling and running. Triathlon is a social group that amplifies certain types of behavior. Triathlon has its own particular nuances, niches and systematic traditions, and in modern English a social group that is defined by its unusual religious, spiritual, or philosophical beliefs or even by its common interest in a particular personality, object, or goal is commonly known as *a cult.*

I totally agree. We will race again.

Acknowledgements

It goes without saying, but I didn't get this far, albeit not that far, without any help and support. The aforementioned individuals mentioned in this book played a key role in shaping the decisions I made and the path I wandered down.

Looking back there must be hundreds of individuals that had given up time to support, volunteer, donate money, and shared advice. I was always aware of this, totally overwhelmed and forever thankful.

I thank my friends and family for not always agreeing that a certain challenge is a great idea, but standing next to my decision, supporting me nonetheless.

A special thanks to my Ironman coach, who saw something in me that maybe no one else did, I certainly didn't. I often remind James that I am eternally grateful for ignoring my lack of confidence and seeing my potential ability.

Last but no means least the biggest acknowledgement and thank you goes to my girlfriend Aoife, with whom I met midway through this existential crisis and in the early stages she had no idea where it was going. Neither did I, but I felt confident in knowing I could seek the unknown and I'd always be loved regardless of the outcome.

Thank you.